STATISTICS

A POCKET GUIDE FOR I/O PSYCHOLOGISTS

©2013

Jeff Foster

Hogan Assessment Systems, Inc.

www.hoganassessments.com

First printing 04-13

ISBN 978-0-9889286-5-7

HOGANPRESS

Table of Contents

Brief Introduction I

Chapter 1 – Statistical Techniques #1 – The Basics

    Topic #1 – Describing Data..3

    Topic #2 – Types of Scales 9

    Topic #3 – Distributions...13

    Topic #4 – Hypothesis Testing...19

    Topic #5 – Reliability..25

    Topic #6 – Validity 29

Chapter 2 – Statistical Techniques #2 – Common Analyses

    Topic #7 – Correlation 35

    Topic #8 – Regression 39

    Topic #9 – T-Test 45

    Topic #10 – Analysis of Variance (ANOVA).....................49

    Topic #11 – Chi-Square 53

Chapter 3 – Statistical Techniques # 3 – More Complex Stuff

    Topic #12 – Exploratory Factor Analysis 59

    Topic #13 – Structural Equation Modeling 67

    Topic #14 – Meta-Analysis 73

    Topic #15 – Mediation & Moderation 79

    Topic #16 – Basics of Item Response Theory (IRT) 83

Chapter 4 – Other Considerations

    Topic #17 – Writing Items..93

    Topic #18 – Translations 97

    Topic #19 – Study Design..101

    Topic #20 – Presenting Your Own Results 105

Index 109

Appendix..111

BRIEF INTRODUCTION

"Lies, damn lies, and statistics"
Benjamin Disraeli – via Mark Twain (and others)

Research and statistical results can be very powerful tools because, simply put, numbers are persuasive. For example, most of us have heard the phrase "the numbers don't lie." Yet, depending on (a) how they are presented, (b) why they are presented, and (c) who is presenting them, numbers can be very misleading.

This can be particularly concerning in the world of I/O Psychology because, within our field, we are often presented with statistical results on a daily basis. Although useful, this can be a problem if we don't understand how to interpret results presented to us or know what questions we should ask to make sure those results are accurate.

As a result, this Pocket Book is a quick reference guide for individuals who are confronted with statistical or research terminology regularly used in I/O Psychology. It provides an overview of common statistical terms, techniques, and processes for your reference. With this information, you can be a better consumer of research results and, therefore, make better data-based decisions.

For more information on any of the topics covered, there are a number of comprehensive texts, instructional guides, and tutorials you can reference. For example, some texts you might find useful include:

> *Statistics in Plain English* (2010 – 3rd Edition) by Timothy Urdan
>
> *Understanding Statistics: A Guide for I/O Psychologists and Human Resource Professionals* (2006) by Michael Aamodt, Michael Surrette, & David Cohen
>
> *Using Multivariate Statistics* (2012 - 6th Edition) by Barbara Tabachnick and Linda Fidell
>
> *Fundamental Statistics for the Behavioral Sciences* (2010) by David Howell
>
> *Test Theory: A Unified Treatment* (2000) by Roderick McDonald

Below are a few key terms to get you started.

Key terms:

- **Construct/Variable** – Anything that varies and can be measured.

- **Measure/Test/Assessment (n.)** – Any scale or set of items intended to assign numerical values to a construct of interest.

- **Items** – The individual items or ratings that comprise a measure, test, or assessment.

- **Scales** – Combinations of items intended to represent a specific construct or variable (e.g., job satisfaction, job performance, general mental ability).

- **Population** – The group or groups of interest in a study.

- **Sample** – Anyone or anything for which a researcher has data.

- **Sample size** – The number of participants or data points in a researcher's sample.

- **Sampling error** – Sampling error is the bane of any researcher, especially those who collect data using human subjects. In general, it means results will vary depending on the subjects available to a researcher simply because no sample can perfectly represent an entire population of interest. For example, one can review exam data from multiple sections of the same Intro to Psychology class and results will differ for no other reason than different students are in different sections. Some will inevitably include students that are more academically inclined than others. One primary goal of many of the statistical tests outlined in Chapters 2 and 3 of this guide are to identify when statistical results (e.g., differences between sections) are simply due to sampling error versus other more important factors (e.g., quality of the instructor).

- **Sample bias** – When statistical results are impacted by characteristics of a sample that do not reflect sampling error. For example, trying to examine the impact of new student orientation training on incoming college freshmen might not generalize to all freshmen if a study just includes data from recent high school graduates (in which case, results might not mean the same thing for non-traditional students).

- **Independent variable** – Inputs or causes (e.g., training, scores on a selection test, developmental feedback). In most studies, a researcher examines the impact of one or more independent variables on outcome or output variables.

- **Dependent variable** – Outcomes or outputs (e.g., learning, job performance, job behaviors).

- **Confounding variables** – Usually unknown variables that impact the relationship between the variables a researcher is interested in studying. They are responsible for a large percentage of the problems we typically see when people present misleading statistical results. Examples of the impact of confounding variables are presented throughout this guide.

Example Variables	Measure	Population	Sample
Test Scores	Number Correct	Stats 101 Students	Results from three sections of Stats 101
Temperature	Degrees Celsius	Average Highs in July	High temperatures throughout a 10 year period
Floor Space	Square feet	Average house size in a neighborhood	Current square footage of 10 houses in the neighborhood

CHAPTER 1

STATISTICAL TECHNIQUES #1 — THE BASICS

The topics covered in this chapter represent the basic foundation of many statistical techniques. Familiarity with the topics and terms outlined throughout this chapter is essential to understanding many of the remaining sections of this guide.

Undergraduate statistical courses cover most of the topics presented in this chapter, although some (e.g., reliability and validity) are often covered in research method courses at both the undergraduate and graduate level. One can conduct the analyses presented in most chapters (e.g., measures of central tendency and variance, presentation of data using histograms, etc.) using common statistical programs such as SPSS, SAS, or even Excel.

TOPIC 1 DESCRIBING DATA

Most basic statistical analyses start the same way – a researcher has some data and wants to describe them (and yes, traditionally, "data" is plural). As the term suggests, **descriptive statistics** help make sense of data and describe them to others.

Descriptive statistics usually pertain to only one variable at a time. For example, in a class setting, that might be overall test scores on a specific exam, or it could be scores on an individual item from that exam. In an organizational setting, that might be average performance ratings, average tenure for a particular job or group of jobs, or the percentage of individuals with incident or accident/injury records over a certain period of time.

Often, one uses descriptive statistics to see how certain measures change over time. For example, do average exam scores increase after a change in teaching style or do accidents and injuries decrease during a 12-month period following safety training?

Key terms:

- **Measures of central tendency** – Measures used to indicate the way in which qualitative data cluster around some value. The three most common measures of central tendency are:

    - **Mean** – The mathematical average. To calculate the mean, add scores on a particular variable and divide by the number of scores you have.

    - **Median** – When one lines up scores in order from lowest to highest, the median is the score that falls in the middle. If there are two scores in the middle (i.e., there is an even number of scores), then most people average those two middle scores to get the median.

    - **Mode** – The score that shows up the most.

- **Median split** – When one divides a set of scores into two groups at the median (i.e., those above the median versus those below the median).

- **Mean Split** – When one divides a set of scores into two groups at the mean (i.e., those above the mathematical average versus those below the mathematical average).

- **Bi- or multi- modal** – When two or more scores that show up the most (i.e., more than one mode).

- **Range** – The difference between the highest and lowest scores on a variable.

- **Interquartile range** – All scores between the 25th and 75th percentiles (see Topic #2 for a description of percentile scores).

- **Variance** – An indication of how spread out results are (i.e., how "varied" they are). To calculate it is a little lengthy, but involves 1) subtracting the mean from each individual value, 2) squaring that result for each individual value, 3) adding up all those squared values, and 4) dividing by the total number of subjects. The important thing to know is that when scores are more spread out, variance will be higher.

- **Standard deviation** – The square root of variance. It is another indication of how much scores vary from one another and serves as the foundation for a number of more complex statistical results covered in later sections.

- **Frequency** – The number of scores falling at a particular value.

- **Relative frequency** – The percentage of scores falling at a particular point.

- **Cumulative frequency** – The percentage of scores falling at or below a particular point.

Examples:

Table 1.1 – Weight of children in a Pre-K class

Student Number	Weight in pounds	Median	Mode	Mean Split	Median Split	Interquartile Range	Difference from the Mean
1	24	24	24	Group 1	Group 1	24	-13
2	26	26	26	Group 1	Group 1	26	-11
3	35	35	35	Group 1	Group 1	35	-2
4	38	38	38	Group 2	Group 1	**38**	1
5	38	38	**38**	Group 2	Group 1	**38**	1
6	38	**38**	**38**	Group 2	Group 1	**38**	1
7	39	**39**	**39**	Group 2	Group 2	**39**	2
8	39	39	39	Group 2	Group 2	**39**	2
9	40	40	40	Group 2	Group 2	**40**	3
10	42	42	42	Group 2	Group 2	42	5
11	42	42	42	Group 2	Group 2	42	5
12	43	43	43	Group 2	Group 2	43	6

Note: scores making up the median, mode, and interquartile range are **bold**.

Mean = sum of all scores divided by the number of scores
= (24+26+35+38+38+38+39+39+40+42+42+43)/12
= (444)/12
= 37.00

Range = largest number minus smallest number
= 43-24
= 19

Variance = first square the difference between each number and the mean and sum them up, then divide by the number of items
= (169+121+4+1+1+1+4+4+9+25+25+37)/12
= (400)/12
= 33.33

Standard Deviation = square root of variance
= Square Root of 33.33
= 5.77

Note: when calculating the standard deviation or variance for a sample, meaning you have data from a limited number of people but want to use that information to generalize to a larger population, you divide by N – 1 rather than N. This is because sample variance tends to be a bit too small compared to a true population. The smaller your sample, the more likely it is that the variance from your sample will underestimate the population variance. So in the example above, if you wanted to use data from your sample to estimate the variance in weights for all Pre-K children, you would divide 400 by 11 rather than 12, resulting in a new variance estimate of 36.36 and new standard deviation estimate of 6.03.

Table 1.2 – Same example as above reported as frequencies

Weight in pounds	Number of Students (frequency)	Relative Frequency	Cumulative Frequency
24	1	8.33%	8.33%
26	1	8.33%	16.67%
35	1	8.33%	25.00%
38	3	25.00%	50.00%
39	2	16.67%	66.67%
40	1	8.33%	75.00%
42	2	16.67%	91.67%
43	1	8.33%	100%
46	1	8.33%	100%

Table 1.3 – Household incomes in the U.S. – 2009

Income level	Relative Frequency	Cumulative Frequency
Under $15K	13.0%	13.0%
$15-25K	11.9%	24.9%
$25-35K	11.1%	36.1%
$35-50K	14.1%	50.2%
$50-75K	18.1%	68.3%
$75-100K	11.5%	79.8%
$100-150K	11.9%	91.8%
$150-200K	4.4%	96.2%
$200K and up	3.8%	100%

Note: Source is the United States Census Bureau at:

http://www.census.gov/compendia/statab/cats/income_
expenditures_poverty_wealth/household_income.html

What to watch for:

One issue that commonly leads to confusion concerns what specific measure of central tendency one uses to report the "average" score for a variable. Even though the mean is technically the average according to most common definitions, people will sometimes call the median the average. So, when someone reports an average score, it never hurts to ask how they came up with that average.

Reported Median = $49,777

Reported Mean = $67,976

When might one want to report the mean as the average? When would one want to report the median instead?

Food for Thought:

Common estimates are that more than half of all traffic accidents take place within 5 miles of a person's home (and over 3/4 occur within 15 miles). Does this mean that people are less likely to drive safely when closer to home?

TOPIC 2 TYPES OF SCALES

There are several different types of scales one can use to collect data. Scale type has important implications for how one collects, analyzes, and reports results. In this section, we cover the most common types of scales used for data collection.

Key terms:

- **Categorical/qualitative data** – Categorical and qualitative data are essentially the same thing. Both terms refer to placing people, subjects, or other constructs of interest into discrete categories (e.g., males versus females, managers versus subordinates, fruits versus vegetables, etc.).

- **Continuous/quantitative data** – Continuous and quantitative data also mean essentially the same thing. Both terms refer to measuring constructs of interest using scales that range from low to high values, such as temperature, height, intelligence, etc.

- **Types of Scales:**

  - **Nominal scale** – Scales that are categorical in nature. As the term suggestion, nominal data involves naming or assigning particular values into discrete categories (e.g., males versus females).

  - **Ordinal scale** – Scales used to rank order sample members on a particular construct, such as the order one finishes in a race. Because ordinal scales usually assign a numeric value to placement (e.g., first, second, etc.), they are typically treated as continuous scales.

  - **Interval scale** – Scales used to assign a specific numerical value to a construct of interest, where values represent equal intervals. Examples are dates, personality measures, and temperature. Interval scales may contain the number zero, but only as an additional point of measurement (i.e., a temperature of zero degrees Celsius does not mean that there is no longer a temperature).

- **Ratio scale** – Similar to interval scales, but the point at which the scale hits zero means there is an absence of what is being measured (e.g., height, weight, number correct on a test, number of days absent from a job).

- **Raw scores** – Numbers assigned to any given attribute. An initial score on any measure is a raw score.

- **Percentile scores** – Provide one means for converting raw scores into a metric that can be used to compare any specific score to others in a sample. Percentile scores are derived from cumulative frequencies (see Topic #1). For example, an individual who weighs the same or more than 3/4 of his or her preschool class is at the 75th percentile.

- **Likert Scale** – Scales often used to collect performance ratings or survey responses from individuals. They have a certain number of points (typically anywhere from 3-10) with lower numbers representing a small degree of or absence of something (e.g., "Strongly Disagree," "Never") and higher numbers representing a large degree or totality of something (e.g., "Strongly Agree," "Always").

Examples:

Table 2.1 – Data collected from a group of call center employees

Empl. #	Age	Gender	# of calls per hour	# of calls converted per week	Rank Order for Conversions	Supervisory Performance Rating
1	23	Male	17	73	3	5 – Exceptional
2	32	Male	23	63	6	2 – Needs Improvement
3	25	Female	8	22	10	1 – Unacceptable
4	27	Female	22	57	7	2 – Needs Improvement
5	23	Male	16	72	4	4 – Strong
6	21	Male	15	53	8	3 – Acceptable
7	22	Female	22	82	1	5 – Exceptional
8	24	Male	27	64	5	4 – Strong
9	23	Female	25	74	2	5 – Exceptional
10	28	Male	17	52	9	3 – Acceptable

Nominal Scales: Employee #, Gender
Ordinal Scale: Rank Order for Conversions
Interval Scale: Supervisory Performance Ratings
Ratio Scales: Age, # of calls per hour, # of calls converted per week

*Note: Assuming Supervisory Performance Ratings were made in the example above using a Likert Scale with endpoints ranging from 1 (Unacceptable) to 5 (Exceptional), most people consider and would treat this as an interval scale. However, some have argued that Likert Scales should be treated as ordinal scale. In reality, however, any differences this might require in terms of statistical calculations are likely to produce only very small differences in results. It is most common, therefore, to treat Likert Scales as interval scales.

What to watch for:

People often make incorrect assumptions because they either don't have all of the data or have mis-interpreted the scale used to collect data. For example:

1. Is it correct to say that individuals with an overall supervisory rating of 3 (Exceptional) are three times better than individuals with an overall rating of 1 (Poor)?

2. Do not make incorrect assumptions based on rank ordering or ordinal scales. Notice that the differences in calls converted from the top to second rated person is a difference of 8 calls per week while the difference between the second and third ranked persons is only 1 call per week.

3. Although the number of calls per hour seems like a fine metric for determining performance, it is insufficient if the company actually cares most about the number of calls that are converted into sales. Notice that Employee #8 makes the most calls per hour, but employee #7 actually converts the most calls into sales.

Food for Thought:

Below is a graph showing the average number of fatal accidents per 1,000 drivers for different age groups. According to these results, teenage drivers are actually safer than people in their early 20's and about equally as safe as people in their late 20's. Yet, anyone with teenage children knows that these differences are not reflected in their insurance premiums. What could be impacting these results to make it appear as though teenagers are safer drivers than individuals in their 20's?

Figure 2.1 – Number of drivers in fatal crashes by age

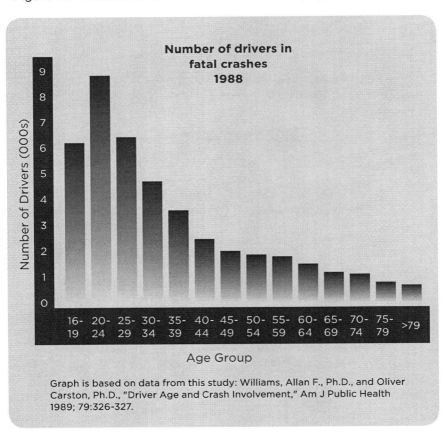

Graph is based on data from this study: Williams, Allan F., Ph.D., and Oliver Carston, Ph.D., "Driver Age and Crash Involvement," Am J Public Health 1989; 79:326-327.

TOPIC 3 DISTRIBUTIONS

Distributions are a collection of scores on a single variable. The term itself is actually very generic and, therefore, can have numerous meanings. Usually, when people refer to a distribution of scores, they are talking about how scores rank from smallest to largest and approximately how many scores fall at specific points or within specific ranges on a variable. One of the most common ways to display a distribution of scores is by using a **Histogram**, which is a method for visually reporting the number of scores (i.e., frequency) falling at specific points or within specific ranges.

Figure 3.1 – Ambition scores for a sample of 30,000+ managers around the world

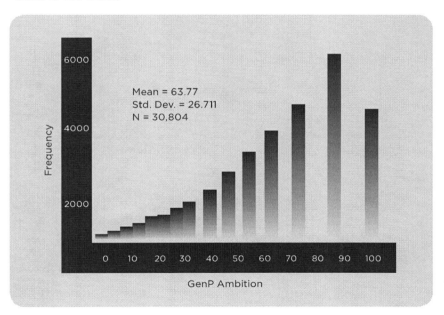

Also, researchers use distributions to show how scores on a variable are expected to fall under certain conditions. The most common example of such a distribution is the **normal distribution**, or **bell curve**.

Figure 3.2 – The Normal Distribution

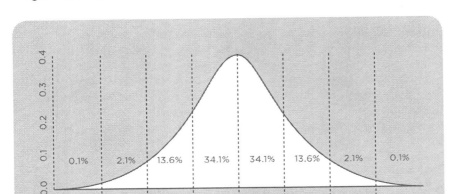

The normal distribution represents data that tend to center around one central value. There are the same number of cases above and below the mean, and fewer cases as a score gets further and further from the mean. This results in a distribution where the mean, median, and mode are all the same value. Many naturally occurring variables tend to follow the normal distribution (e.g., height and weight, blood pressure, most standardized test scores).

Key Terms:

- **z-score** – Represents the number of standard deviations a particular score is away from the mean. For example, if the mean score on an assessment center is 25 and the standard deviation is 3, a raw score of 28 would be the equivalence of a z-score of 1.00 (and a raw score of 22 would be a z-score of -1.00).

- **Standardized score** – Represents a wide variety of scoring methods used to convert an individual raw score into something that can be more readily compared to other scores from a sample or population. By themselves, raw scores don't always carry a lot of meaning unless one knows the scale's average and standard deviation.

- **Outlier** – Any extreme score. For example, if the average score on a math exam is 80 out of 100, an individual receiving a 20 out of 100 is likely an outlier. Outliers are often identified as any score falling more than 2 or 3 standard deviations away from the mean.

- **Skew/Skewness** – The degree to which one tail of a distribution is longer than the other. For example, household incomes in the U.S. are often skewed, with most people falling around the mathematical average of around $35-75K and only a small percentage falling well above that average in the $200K+ range.

- **Kurtosis** – An indication of how tall or flat a distribution is. When most scales fall around the mean, the distribution appears tall and is called "leptokurtic." When scores are very spread out, the distribution appears more flat and called "platykurtic."

Examples:

Below are examples of two common types of standardized scores. With Sten scores, individuals receive a score of 1-10 on a variable based on their z-score on that variable. Stanine scores are very similar but are on a 1-9 scale. For example, if a person's score on a variable is 0.60 standard deviations above the mean on a variable, their sten score score would be 7 (out of 10) and their Stanine score would be 6 (out of 9). A score that is 1.60 standard deviations below the mean would receive both a Sten and Stanine score of 2.

Table 3.1 – Sten Scores

Sten	1	2	3	4	5	6	7	8	9	10
Z-scores	< -2.0	-2 to -1.5	-1.5 to -1.0	-1.0 to -.5	-.5 to 0	0 to +.5	+.5 to +1.0	+1.0 to +1.5	+1.5 to +2.0	> +2.0
Percent	2.3%	4.4%	9.2%	15.0%	19.2%	19.2%	15.0%	9.2%	4.4%	2.3%
Sten score	0	1	2	3	4	5	6	7	8	9

Table 3.1 – Sten Scores

Stanine	1	2	3	4	5	6	7	8	9	10
Standard score	below -1.75	-1.75 to -1.25	-1.25 to -.75	-.75 to -.25	-.25 to +.25	+.25 to +.75	+.75 to +1.25	+1.25 to +1.75	above +1.75	> +2.0
Percent	4%	7%	12%	17%	20%	17%	12%	7%	4%	2.3%
Sten score	0	1	2	3	4	5	6	7	8	9

The following figure presents an example of a normal curve (in blue) and a positively skewed curve (in red). Notice that the skew is positive because there are a handful of scores stretched out at the positive end of the scale. That does not necessarily mean that scores on the scale are higher on average.

Figure 3.3 – A normal and positively skewed distribution.

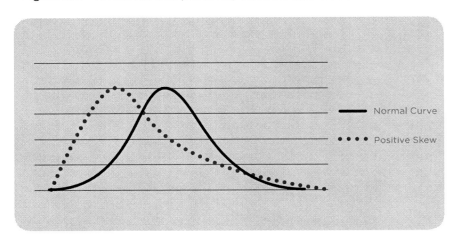

What to watch for:

Standard scores often mean very little unless one knows the measure's mean and standard deviation. For example, without knowing that average SAT scores are approximately 500, there is no way of knowing if a score of 400 is above or below average.

Also, outliers and/or skewness can dramatically impact measures of central tendency. For example, consider a class of 10 students who have a mean score of 80 out of 100 on an exam. If you replace just one person with a score of 90 and substitute in another student with a score of 10, that mean score will drop to 72 simply because of that one change (although the median is likely to only change by a couple of points, if at all).

Food for Thought:

Climate change continues to be a hot topic in environmental, scientific, and political arenas. Both proponents and detractors of major climate change regularly throw out numbers to support their claims. For example, recent statistics indicate that 2012 was the hottest year in U.S. history. Yet, there are thousands of examples of different U.S. cities hitting new record lows for specific dates throughout the year. How is this possible?

TOPIC 4 HYPOTHESIS TESTING

Hypotheses are just research questions one tests through various statistical methods. There are two primary types of hypotheses. The first is the **Null Hypothesis**, which typically states there is no difference between groups on a particular measure or no relationship between multiple measures. Ironically, it is the null hypothesis we actually test with statistics, even though we usually expect an alternative hypothesis to be true. An **Alternative Hypothesis** typically states there are differences between groups or that multiple measures are associated with one other. If statistical results indicate we can likely reject the null hypothesis, then we have evidence that at least one alternative hypothesis is likely true. Along those lines, we can have more than one alternative hypothesis.

For example, consider a test of whether or not computerized instruction leads to greater learning, as measured by a post-training exam, as compared to traditional classroom-based instruction. To examine this question, a researcher randomly assigns two class sections to receive classroom-based instruction and two classes to receive training via a new computerized course.

> Null Hypothesis (often designated as H_0): Scores on the post training exam will be the same regardless of instructional method.

> Alternative Hypothesis #1 (often designated as H_1): Scores on the post training exam will be higher for those who received computerized instruction compared to those who received traditional classroom-based instruction.

> Alternative Hypothesis #2 (or H_2): Scores on the post training exam will be higher for those who received traditional classroom-based instruction compared to those who received computerized instruction.

Key terms:

- **Inferential statistics** – Any statistical method that allows a researcher to make inferences about a sample or population. For example, when a survey company polls 500 likely voters from a district, they use these results to infer how all voters in the district are likely to vote on election-day.

- **Statistical significance** – The probability, from 0 to 100 percent, that any observed differences between groups on a measure or association between multiple measures is due to chance.

- **Alpha** – The statistic most often tied to significance tests. Alphas range from 0.00 to 1.00. These scores represent the likelihood (i.e., percent chance) that an alternative hypothesis is true. Typically, alphas of .05 or less are interpreted as "statistically significant." This means there is less than a 5% chance that any difference between groups or association between measures is simply due to chance.

- **Practical significance** – Whether or not a difference between groups on a measure or association between variables is practically meaningful.

- **Effect size** – The magnitude of the difference between groups on a measure or the magnitude of the association between multiple measures.

- **One-tailed v. Two-tailed test** – One-tailed tests are tests that an effect occurs in a specific direction (e.g., group 1 scores are higher than group 2 or two variables are associated so that, as values on one increase, values on the other also increase). Two-tailed tests are tests that an effect is significant but could be in either direction (e.g., either group could be higher than the other or two measures are significantly associated with one another, but as one increases, the other could either increase or decrease).

- **Type 1 error** – Rejecting a null hypothesis that is actually true. In other words, it is when a researcher finds a random difference or association that is purely due to chance, but large enough they conclude it must be real. The smaller one's alpha, the less likely they are to commit a type 1 error.

- **Type 2 error** – The failure to reject a null hypothesis that is false. In other words, the difference or association a researcher is testing might be real, but it either doesn't show up in their data due to chance and/or their sample is too small to examine the effect they are trying to test.

- **Power** – The chances of avoiding a type 2 error. Power increases as (a) the magnitude of an effect increases and (b) sample size increases. In other words, the larger an effect and sample size, the higher one's power (i.e., the less likely they are to commit a type 2 error).

- **Degrees of freedom** – Technically speaking, the number of values in a statistical calculation that are free to vary. For many simple statistical tests, degrees of freedom equals one's sample size minus one. But, it can be sample size minus more than one for more complex analyses, such as those covered in Chapter 3.

Examples:

One could produce a longer more complex list of hypotheses by adding a third group (e.g., simply asking another two "classes" to learn their material by reading a text book). With the introduction of such a third condition, various hypotheses could include no differences across the three conditions, that one instructional method would work better than the other two, that one would not work as well as the other two, or that average scores would follow some specified order (e.g., computer instruction would work best, followed by classroom-based instruction, followed by reading a text book).

Furthermore, when one tests a hypothesis concerning group differences, they never expect results to be exactly equal across groups. Consider the example above. It is very unlikely (and would be rare) that the mean exam scores for those in both instructional conditions would be exactly the same. Researchers often try to minimize unintentional differences between groups by randomly assigning study participants to our various conditions. But when they still find differences, statistical analyses help determine the **probability**, or likelihood, that these differences are due to chance rather than true differences between conditions (e.g., that computerized instruction really did work better).

The same is true when one looks for associations between multiple measures. For example, they could examine if there is a relationship between time spent studying and post-training exam scores. In this case, their null hypothesis would be that time spent studying and exam scores are not related. Their alternative would likely be that, as time spent studying increases, exam scores also tend to increase. Again, they are likely to find some small association between any two measures simply due to chance. Statistical analyses help determine how likely it is that this association is due to real relationships between the measures they are examining.

What to watch for:

For most significance tests, alpha is impacted by sample size. This means that the larger one's sample, the lower one's alpha. As a result, when a researcher has huge samples, alpha is almost always less than .05. However, in such cases, even though they likely have a difference that is not due simply to chance, it doesn't mean that difference is practically meaningful. For example, consider the hypotheses outlined above, but this time tested on 100 classes who received computerized instruction (with an average score of 16.5 out of 20) and 100 classes who received classroom based instruction (with an average score of 16.8 out of 20). The difference of 0.3 might be statistically significant, but if the classroom instruction is more time consuming and expensive, the average increase of only 0.3 might not be worth the extra money and resources required for so many classes.

Also, there continues to be a lot of debate concerning the nature of hypothesis testing. Much of this debate centers on the emphasis of testing null hypotheses, which many have argued are almost never true. After all, why would someone spend time and effort examining a potential effect if it doesn't exist? As a result, the failure to reject a null hypothesis is often the result of small sample sizes or poorly designed studies. More importantly, many researchers make the mistake of concluding a null hypothesis is true if results indicate they should not reject it. Technically speaking, we can never conclude that a null hypothesis is true or false. We can only use significance tests to determine the probability it is false given our data. Still, a significance test itself is often helpful because it is an objective estimate of how likely results are due to chance. Although it says nothing about the quality of measures or research design, it does provide a means of putting results into perspective.

Food for Thought:

There continues to be a lot of debate over published studies in well respected journals that find significant effects for various forms of extra-sensory perception. For example, consider a study by Daryl Bern at Cornell published in the Journal of Personality and Social Psychology in 2011. It presented evidence of pre-cognition, or the ability to see into the future (to at least some degree). This study examined something familiar to all of us, which is that we remember words better when we rehearse their meanings. Of course, this typically means we rehearse the words before we are tested. In his study, however, Dr. Bern found that subjects tested better on word meanings even if they rehearsed them *after* they were tested (as opposed to no rehearsal after testing). To perhaps no one's surprise, several attempts to replicate these findings resulted in a failure to reject the null hypothesis (i.e., no significant effects of post-testing rehearsal). Of perhaps bigger concern, however, is that at least some have claimed that attempts to publish their non-significant findings met with failure, even in the same journal. Why might that be the case and what are the bigger implications concerning results we see on a daily basis, even in academic outlets?

TOPIC 5 RELIABILITY

In general, **reliability** refers to how consistent scores are across multiple ratings or rating sources. In other words, if a researcher tries to measure the same thing multiple times or measure it using multiple methods, how similar are his or her results?

There are several types of reliability that are calculated in different ways, but in general, most result in scores that range from 0.00 (representing no reliability – or no consistency/agreement) to 1.00 (representing perfect reliability). Reliability scores greater than .90 are usually considered very good, whereas scores that range anywhere from .60 to .70 or higher are often considered adequate. Granted, it all depends on the purpose of the measure and the type of reliability one computes, but a researcher can generally expect to raise eyebrows when any reliability coefficient falls below.60 or .50.

Key terms:

- **True score** – A hypothetical value of exactly what a score would be if it were measured perfectly.

- **Observed score** – The result a researcher gets when measuring something. An observed score is comprised of both a true score and error.

- **Error** – Anything that impacts a measure to cause the result to deviate from a true score. As error increases, reliability decreases. Error can result from a wide range of issues, such as problems with the measure itself (e.g., a short and inaccurate IQ test), unforeseen variables that impact the measure (e.g., how much sleep the person got the night before taking an IQ test), or an actual error (e.g., failing to properly record a person's results on an IQ test).

- **Standard error of measurement** – A calculation used to determine how accurate an observed score is likely to be (e.g., how close an observed score is likely to be to the underlying true score of interest).

- **Standard error of the mean** – Similar to standard error of measurement but, as the name suggests, applied to the mean score from an entire sample rather than each individual score. In other words, it is used to determine how likely an observed mean is to a group's true mean if the construct of interest could have been measured perfectly (i.e., without error).

- **Confidence interval** – A range in which a true score is likely to fall. For example, if a person's score on a comprehensive and highly reliable IQ test is 100, one could use the standard error of measurement associated with the test to calculate a 95% confidence interval (e.g., there is a 95% chance that their "true" IQ is between 97 and 103). However, with a less reliable test, the confidence interval may be much larger (e.g., could be as large as 80 to 120 if reliability is low).

Examples:

- **Split Forms reliability** – A reliability estimate derived from splitting a test in half and correlating scores on both halves with one another.

- **Coefficient (or Cronbach's) Alpha** – A measure of internal consistency, or to what degree a set of items generally measure the same construct of interest (see more below).

- **Test-Retest reliability** – The correlation between test scores measured at two different points in time.

- **Parallel Forms reliability** – The correlation between two sets of items designed to be as identical to one another as possible (i.e., measure the same construct with the same degree of difficulty).

- **Kuder-Richardson Formula (KR-20)** – A short formula for estimating what coefficient alpha would be if items were added to or removed from a scale.

What to Watch For:

When someone asks what the reliability of a measure is, they are often asking about coefficient alpha. Coefficient alpha is commonly referred to as a measure of internal consistency. In general, that means to what degree items on a scale measure the same thing. For example, if a researcher is measuring how extraverted (i.e., outgoing and social) others are, the researcher might ask his or her subjects several items such as whether they like going to parties, like large crowds, or are often the first to speak at meetings. People who say yes to any one of these items are probably more likely to say yes to one or more other items because, if written well, all items should generally get at the same thing: how outgoing and social a person is. The more items the researcher writes, and the better those items get at extraversion, the higher his or her coefficient alpha will be.

Perhaps because it is so common, coefficient alpha is also frequently misused. The most common misuse is calculating an alpha on a set of items that were never intended to measure the same construct. For example, many personality assessments contain items representing multiple scales such as extraversion (outgoing and social), conscientiousness (rule abiding and hard working), and openness (open to new experiences and ideas). When an assessment contains more than one scale, it is only appropriate to calculate alpha on each scale individually, not across all scales or sets of items intended to measure different constructs.

Along those same lines, individual scales intended to predict some sort of outcome (e.g., job performance) might be comprised of items that measure different things (e.g., drive, experience, IQ). Such scales are **multi-dimensional** in that they are comprised of items deliberately intended to measure different things. Again, coefficient alpha is an inappropriate estimate of reliability for these scales. Instead, some alternative form of reliability, such as test-retest, should be used. In contrast, test-retest might be inappropriate for examining scales that measure any construct that changes over time (e.g., mood at any one particular point in time). The main thing to keep in mind is the nature of the scale and its intended use dictates which form or forms of reliability are most appropriate.

Food for Thought:

Consider an example where a researcher wants to develop a measure of teamwork. They write the following five items and ask supervisors to rate 100 different employees on each item (using a 5-point Likert Scale where 1 indicates "strongly disagree" and 5 indicates "strongly agree").

This employee:

1. Is friendly and cooperative.

2. Helps other when needed.

3. Is a good team member.

4. Works well in a team.

5. Gets along well with everyone.

They analyze their data and find a coefficient alpha of .60. Not bad, but not as high as they had hoped. Through some fancy reliability analyses in SPSS where they asked what alpha would be if specific items were removed, they conclude that they could reach an alpha of .80 with only items 3 and 4. Even though the alpha would be higher, would this result in a better overall measure of teamwork?

TOPIC 6 VALIDITY

Researchers have tried to come up with a consistent and comprehensive definition of validity for decades. No one has. However, in the most general sense, **validity** is usually meant as an indication of whether or not, or to what degree, a measurement does what it is supposed to. **Validation** is the process one uses to try to estimate or establish validity.

If one calculates reliability properly (see Topic #5), it is not possible to have validity without reliability. In other words, if any measure is wildly inconsistent (i.e., low reliability), then it probably isn't of much use (i.e., low validity). However, a measure can have high reliability but still have little to no validity. For example, you could use a tape measure to assess the distance between a person's front door and the street. If used correctly, you should get almost the exact same measurement over and over again as this distance is unlikely to change over short periods of time. In other words, it would be very reliable. But it isn't going to be a valid measure of anything other than the distance from their front door to the street.

Key terms:

- **Predictor variable** – The variable that, one generally assumes, impacts results on another variable. Predictor variables are independent variables intended to predict some outcome of interest. For example, does IQ (a predictor variable) impact job performance?

- **Criterion/Outcome variable** – The variable a researcher wants to predict or influence (e.g., job performance). Criterion variables are dependent variables that represent some specific outcome of interest.

- **Utility** – The result of implementing a predictor variable to influence an outcome of interest. In I/O Psychology, utility typically refers to the benefit a company gets out of using some sort of predictor variable (e.g., interview rating, assessment tests) to select new employees.

- **Utility Analysis** – A procedure for estimating the utility of some HR related activity (e.g., a selection test, training) in terms of some metric of interest (e.g., profit, productivity, days lost, or turnover). Generally, the more predictive a selection procedure or effective some other HR intervention, the higher its utility; although the costs of implementing the procedure must also be taken into account.

Examples:

- **Face validity** – Whether or not a measure looks as if it measures what it is supposed to. In other words, does a set of items seem to match their intended purpose? For example, job interviews may have face validity as long as the questions asked seem job-related. However, questions like "If you could be any kind of tree, what kind of tree would you be?" tend to have lower face validity (and consequently, don't predict job performance as well).

- **Content validity** – To what degree a scale represents the full construct it is intended to measure. For example, an emotional intelligence assessment only has content validity to the degree to which it measures all of the different components of emotional intelligence (e.g., identifying emotions in self and others, controlling emotions in self and others).

- **Construct validity** – Although frequently referenced, "construct validity" is a term that unfortunately lacks a clear or agreed upon definition. Usually it refers to how well a measure correlates with a theoretical construct it is intended to measure. In other words, does it measure what it is actually supposed to? Some have called construct validity the only true form of validity whereas others have went so far as to discard it completely, saying that it is not a useful concept because there is no agreed upon definition of what it even means. Still, a generally recognized method of trying to assess construct validity is by examining correlations between a target measure and other measures, paying particular attention to two types of relationships that are commonly defined through two other validity-related terms:

- **Convergent validity** – To what degree a measure correlates with other similar measures (i.e., those intended to measure similar constructs).

- **Discriminant validity** – To what degree a measure does not correlate with measures intended to assess different constructs.

- **Criterion-Related validity** – The extent to which a score on one measure predicts a score on some criterion or outcome measure. This is usually determined by correlating scores on a predictor measure (e.g., interview scores from job applicants) with scores relating to an outcome of interest (e.g., job performance ratings collected at a later date).

  - **Predictive validity** – A criterion-related validity study when predictor measures are collected from job applicants and job performance ratings are collected at a later point in time (e.g., once those hired have been on the job for one year).

  - **Concurrent validity** – Similar to predictive validity, but scores on the predictor measure are collected from existing employees rather than applicants. Because it is often difficult to spend the time and money on a potential selection instrument without actually using it for some period of time so data can be collected to assess predictive validity (i.e., wait long enough until job applicants have been hired and on the job for a year or two), concurrent validity is often used as a quicker and less expensive alternative.

- **Internal validity** – Deals with the accuracy of results from a research study (e.g., does a relationship between IQ and classroom performance for one individual class represent a true relationship or is it only due to chance?).

- **External validity** – Deals with the degree to which results from one study should generalize to similar samples (e.g., can one expect the same relationship to be true for other classes?).

What to Watch For:

People misuse the term "validity" all the time. Because related terms such as "valid" and "validate" are commonly used in everyday life, it is easy to see why validity is so often misused in the realm of research and statistics. Therefore, when hearing someone refer to validity, it is important to make sure you (and possibly the other person) understand what they mean when they use the term.

Food for Thought:

Perhaps one of the most widely used self-proclaimed personality tests in the world is the Oxford Capacity Analysis (OCA). The Church of Scientology uses this assessment in many of its recruiting efforts. Many in the "scientific" community have criticized it as not being a genuine personality test. Along those lines, several attempts to collect data using the OCA for the purposes of "validating" it as a personality assessment have fallen short. Yet, proponents still claim it is valid (or simply do not care about claims that it is not). Is it possible that individuals on both sides of this debate are correct?

CHAPTER 2

STATISTICAL TECHNIQUES #2 — COMMON ANALYSES

This chapter covers basic statistical techniques commonly used in I/O Psychology for simple comparisons between variables or to compare scores from one group to one or more other groups. These statistical techniques are typically covered in both undergraduate and graduate level statistics classes.

And, as long as you understand the basic information covered in this chapter, a quick Google search of the topic should provide dozens of examples and walkthroughs of how to quickly and easily complete these analyses. Like many of the topics covered in Chapter 1, the topics in this chapter can be quickly conducted using common statistical packages like SPSS, SAS and, often with just a little more work, in Excel.

TOPIC 7 CORRELATION

Correlation is a statistical technique (or technically, a set of techniques) used to examine the degree of association between two measures. Correlation is probably the most common statistical technique used in I/O Psychology. Essentially, a correlation is a measure of **association**, meaning it tells us to what degree scores on one variable tend to increase (or decrease) as scores increase on another variable. Correlations do not, however, imply **causation**. In other words, one cannot assume based on a correlation that changes in one variable actually cause changes in another.

Correlations are reported using values that range from -1.00 (for a perfect negative relationship – meaning that as values on one variable increase, values on the other decrease) to 1.00 (for a perfect positive relationship – meaning that as values on one variable increase, values on the other variable also increase). A correlation of 0.00 indicates two variables are not associated with one another at all. The symbol for a correlation coefficient is "r".

One common example of a correlation is height and weight. As people's height increases, their weight also tends to increase, although this relationship is not a perfect correlation (it is actually around $r = .70$). This suggests that taller people tend to weigh more, but not universally. It is certainly possible for someone who is six feet tall to weigh less than someone who is five feet tall. But on average, people who are taller tend to weigh more.

Squaring a correlation often makes the result easier to interpret because a squared correlation (*r-squared* or r^2) indicates the percentage of variance accounted for in one variable by the other. To illustrate, consider the height and weight example where r^2 =.49 (e.g., .70 x .70). This indicates that approximately half of the fluctuation in people's weight is accounted for by their height while the remaining 51% is accounted for by other factors such as diet, exercise, genetics, etc. Granted, this phrase is a little misleading because it seems to imply causation even though we know we cannot determine causation from correlation. So, even though a more appropriate definition of r^2 would be something like "percentage of variance shared between variables," "percentage of variance accounted for" is still the phrase most commonly used to describe r^2.

There are several ways to calculate a correlation. For the most part, they differ depending on what types of scales are used to measure variables of interest (e.g., ordinal, interval or ratio scales). Most statistical programs automatically use the appropriate type of calculation based on the measures under examination. With correlation, we also get one alpha (see Topic #4) score that helps us determine if the association we find between variables is likely due to chance. This test for statistical significance is determined by both the magnitude of a relationship and sample size. So with a stronger relationship and a larger sample, alpha decreases (meaning it is less likely that results are simply due to chance).

Key terms:

- **Covariance** – Another indication of the degree to which two measures are associated with one another. A correlation coefficient is essentially just covariance that has been converted into a -1.00 to 1.00 score.

- Common types of correlations:

  - **Person product-moment** – Used to calculate a correlation between two quantitative (i.e., interval or ratio) scales.

  - **Spearman's rho** – Used to calculate a correlation between two ordinal scales

  - **Point-biserial** – Used to calculate a correlation between one nominal and one quantitative scale.

  - **Phi Coefficient** – Used to calculate a correlation between two nominal scales.

Examples:

Correlations can often be seen and understood best through **scatter plots**, which are graphical representations of where scores for individual subjects fall on the two measures under examination. Some examples include:

Figure 7.1 – Examples of scatter plots representing different correlations

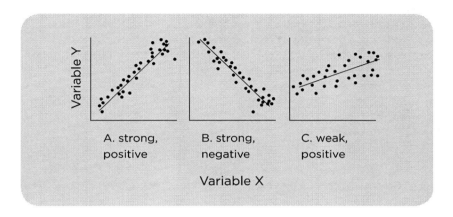

A. strong, positive   B. strong, negative   C. weak, positive

Variable X

What to Watch For:

Small correlations are not necessarily unimportant. As with other types of statistics, the practical importance of any result depends on what is being examined. Typically, correlations around .10 are considered small, those around .30 are considered moderate, and those of .50 or higher are considered strong. However, even small correlations might have practical significance.

In I/O Psychology, one of the most common uses of correlations is to examine relationships between scores on a selection measure (e.g., interviews, assessment centers, cognitive ability tests, personality measures) and job performance. For the most part, even the most predictive selection measures are only correlated with job performance at around .20-.30. However, correlations as small as .10 for any one selection measure can be the difference between hiring a high potential job applicant versus one that is less likely to do well on the job.

One factor that can dramatically impact a correlation is **range restriction**, meaning that a researcher does not have a full range of scores on one or both variables under examination. Range restriction usually reduces the size of a correlation if one only has data from subjects at one end or another on either variable. For example, the correlation between height and weight for preschoolers is likely less than .70. However, examining data from groups only at both extreme ends on a variable can artificially increase a correlation. If one were to examine the correlation between height and weight for preschoolers and NBA players, all included in the same set of data, the result would likely be much higher than .70. So, always be sure to interpret correlations with range restriction in mind. Again, missing data at either the low end or high end of a scale will artificially decrease the size of a correlation. Missing data in the middle will artificially increase the size of the correlation.

Food for Thought:

One topic that has received a lot of media attention over the last decade is the potential link between autism and vaccinations. As the number of children receiving vaccinations has steadily increased over the years, the number of children diagnosed with autism has also increased (i.e., the two are clearly correlated). Yet, a number of published scientific studies find no direct link between the two, leading many prominent sources such as the CDC, the World Health Organization, the American Academy of Pediatrics, and even the Autism Science Foundation to state there is currently no evidence that vaccinations are directly linked to autism. How is this possible?

For a less serious example, consider the fact that, as the number of churches in a town increases, the number of bars usually increases as well. In other words, the two are highly correlated. However, despite the many off color explanations of this relationship we might be able to come up with, there is no clear reason to believe that going to church makes one more likely to frequent bars, or the other way around. Yet, the correlation between the two is real. How is this possible?

Finally, consider an example where someone administers 100 potential predictor items to 200 job incumbents and examines the relationships between each item and job performance ratings. They find that 20 items are significantly related to job performance. Furthermore, they create a scale by summing scores on these 20 items and find that results correlate with job performance at .40. This correlation is much higher than correlations between nearly any selection measure and job performance. Why might this be the case?

TOPIC 8 REGRESSION

Regression builds off of correlation but usually involves associating multiple predictor variables with one criterion/outcome variable of interest. The resulting statistic (MR) ranges from 0.00 (no association between the outcome variable and any other predictor variable) to 1.00 (the outcome variable can be perfectly predicted by one or more predictor variables). Like r with correlation, one can square MR to determine the percentage of variance in an outcome measure that is accounted for by a combination of all predictor measures.

Furthermore, regression provides weights for each predictor variable. These weights represent how predictors can be combined to account for the largest percentage of variance possible in the outcome variable of interest. In other words, they represent how predictors can be combined to create a new predictor scale (see example below) that is most highly correlated with the outcome of interest. Furthermore, comparing these weights to one another helps identify which variables are most predictive of the outcome.

Regression results can be illustrated using an equation, usually something similar to $\hat{y} = a + b_1 x$. In this equation, $\hat{y}$ is the predicted value of y, which represents the outcome variable of interest. So, y represents actual values on the outcome and $\hat{y}$ represents predicted values based on x, which is a person's score on a predictor variable. The other two components of the equation are a and b_1, where a represents an **intercept**, or $\hat{y}$ when x = 0, and b_1 represents the **slope** of x, or incremental increases in $\hat{y}$ with each one point increase in x. See the example below for a better illustration of this equation.

As mentioned, regression can include more than one predictor variable. The resulting equation is very similar but has additional components for each additional predictor variable (e.g., $\hat{y} = a + b_1 x + b_2 z$). In this case, z is the second predictor variable and b_2 represents its slope. In instances involving more than one predictor variable, the intercept (a) is the predicted value of y ($\hat{y}$) when both predictor variables (x and z) equal zero.

Like correlation, regression produces alphas to help determine if the association between variables is likely due to chance. And like correlation, these tests for statistical significance are determined by both the magnitude of the relationships and sample size. So with stronger relationships and larger samples, alpha decreases (meaning it is less likely that results are simply due to chance). With only one predictor variable, regression provides only one alpha. But with more than one predictor, regression provides an alpha associated with the entire equation (i.e., what is the likelihood that the relationship between all predictors, when combined, and the outcome is simply due to chance) and for each individual predictor variable (i.e., what is the likelihood that the contribution to prediction of each predictor is simply due to chance).

Key terms:

- **Simple regression** – Very similar to correlation in that there is only one predictor. So, like correlation, there are only two variables: one predictor and one outcome. One advantage of simple regression over correlation is that it can be used to create a regression line with both an intercept and slope. One can then use this line to graphically represent the relationship between the two variables.

- **Multiple regression** – Regression involving more than one predictor variable (but still only one outcome variable).

- **Beta weight** – A standardized slope or regression weight, meaning what the slope would be if all variables were first standardized (see Topic #3). The advantage of beta weights is that they put all predictors on a common metric so that they can be more easily compared to one another.

- **Stepwise regression** – A series of methods used to determine which predictors to include in a regression model. Stepwise regression is useful when a researcher has a lot of potential predictor variables but wants to identify a small set that most effectively predict an outcome variable. It involves different procedures for including only variables that are most predictive and excluding those that no longer help predict the outcome variable once other predictors are already included in the model.

- **Covariates/Control variables** – Variables that are associated with an outcome of interest but whose influence a researcher wants to remove from analyses so he or she can more clearly see the relationship between other variables of interest. For example, if one wanted to determine the impact of education level on annual income, he or she might first want to "control" for other variables that also impact income such as age and parents socioeconomic status. When treating age and socioeconomic status as control variables, regression statistically removes their effect on income, so what is left is a better indication of the true relationship between just education and income.

- **Dummy variables** – Categorical variables can be used as predictors in regression, but only when first converted into dummy variables. Dummy variables have only two potential values: 0 and 1. Each dummy variable represents membership into only one potential group on its associated categorical variable. For a categorical variable, regression requires a dummy variable for all but one group. So, if a researcher is examining the relationship between political affiliation and knowledge of U.S. history, he or she would first have to code people by political affiliation (e.g., republican, democrat, independent, or other). To include this variable in a regression equation, three dummy variables are required (e.g., one containing values of 1 for all republicans and 0 for everyone else, one containing values of 1 for every democrat and 0 for everyone else, and one containing values of 1 for all independents and everyone else). The resulting regression weights associated with each dummy variable help determine if being part of that specific group (e.g., republican, democrat, or independent) affects the outcome of interest.

- **Logistic regression** – A related but separate procedure used to predict a categorical outcome variable. In other words, it provides information concerning how likely individual subjects are to fit into specific groups on an outcome variable based on scores on any number of predictor variables.

- **Hierarchical regression** – Regression involving multiple variables entered into a regression equation through a series of steps. This approach helps determine if variables entered during later steps are associated with an outcome of interest even after having already entered other predictor variables in earlier steps. For example, say a researcher has success predicting job performance with scores on a cognitive ability test, a personality test, and an interview, but wants to see if prediction can be further increased by including scores from an assessment center. He or she would enter the first three predictor variables into the first step of a hierarchical regression equation and then enter assessment center results into step 2. A significant increase in prediction from step 1 to step 2 would indicate that assessment center results likely increases prediction above and beyond the original three predictors. Hierarchical regression is necessary for testing covariates (all of which have to be entered before entering predictor variables) and other relationships between variables such as interactions (see Topic #10) and curvilinear relationships (see below).

- **Change in R-Square** – Hierarchical regression produces not only alphas associated with each step but an alpha representing changes in prediction from one step to the next. This indicates whether new variables significantly predict an outcome variable even after other variables have been entered in previous steps. This is often called **incremental validity** (e.g., does an assessment center have incremental validity over the other three variables in the example above, meaning does it predict job performance "above and beyond" the other three variables, or after the effects of the other variables "have already been taken into account").

- **Curvilinear relationships** – Correlation and most simple regression analyses examine linear relationships between variables, or relationships that are a straight line such as the relationship between height and weight. However, some relationships might be non-linear, such as the relationship between tenure and the performance of athletes. For the most part, athletes tend to get better as they get more experience, but if they stay healthy long enough, their performance will eventually start to decrease as they age.

It is possible to test for such relationships using regression. To do so, one first squares the predictor variable of interest (e.g., tenure). The next step is to enter the original predictor into a hierarchical regression equation as step 1 and then its squared value as step 2. If the alpha associated with the change in R-square for step 2 is significant, there is evidence of a curvilinear relationship. The resulting regression line can then be used to plot this relationship for easier interpretation.

Examples:

To illustrate how a regression equation ($\hat{y} = a + b_yx$) works, consider an example where a researcher uses years of experience to predict job performance. One might assume that job performance increases to some degree with experience, but it is certainly not a perfect relationship, as job performance is also impacted by a number of additional factors. In this case, y is job performance (measured on a 0-100 scale with an average score of 50) and x is years of experience (which ranges from 0 to 40 years). Based on data from 100 people, the resulting regression equation is $\hat{y} = 40 + 0.5x$. The best predicted value for individuals with zero years of experience ($x = 0$) is designated by the intercept, which equals 40. So, people with no job experience tend to, on average, receive job performance ratings of 40 out of 100. Next, the slope (b_y) equals 0.5. This indicates that average job performance tends to increase 0.5 points for every one year of experience. So, if one wants to predict job performance for someone who has been on the job for 24 years (i.e., determine $\hat{y}$ when x equals 24), the result would be $\hat{y} = 40 + 0.5*24 = 52$.

One could then expand on this equation by adding another variable: cognitive ability. Assume that cognitive ability also predicts job performance, and that ratings (represented by z, based on a test with a 0-100 score) are available for all 100 people in the sample. The resulting multiple regression equation is now $\hat{y} = 20 + 0.3x + 0.45z$. Notice that when including cognitive ability, both the intercept and the slope for experience changes. And, because there are now multiple predictor variables that are related to the outcome variable, prediction also increases. So, to predict job performance for someone who has been on the job for 10 years and had a cognitive ability score of 85 out of 100, the result would be $\hat{y} = 20 + 0.3*10 + 0.45*85 = 61.25$.

What to Watch For:

One common concern with regression is known as **multicolinearity**, which essentially just means there can be problems when one or more predictor variables are strongly correlated with one another. Using multiple predictors that are highly related often doesn't help prediction. For example, if adding two additional cognitive ability measures into the example above, the new measures would likely add little value in helping better predict job performance (assuming the first cognitive ability measure is a good one). But, because they are highly correlated, the resulting slopes associated with each would be very unstable, meaning that just adding or subtracting one or two people from the sample could completely change the slopes for each of the three cognitive ability measures.

Like correlation, regression only analyzes associations between variables. It does not imply causation. Although when speaking of regression, researchers often use terms like "predictor variables" and "outcome variables," that does not necessarily mean predictors actually cause changes in outcomes of interest.

Food for Thought:

Some have claimed that one's job performance can be predicted through two unrelated types of intelligence: traditional IQ and emotional intelligence (EI or EQ). Because we know IQ generally accounts for about 15% of the variance in job performance ratings, some proponents of EQ have claimed that EQ must, therefore, account for the remaining 85%. What is wrong with this claim?

TOPIC 9 T-TEST

T-tests (or student's t-tests) represent a common and simple method used to determine if average scores on an outcome variable for one group are statistically different from scores on the same outcome variable for another group.

T-tests may be conducted on one sample, such as when a group's mean is compared to a larger sample of means. This is called a **one-sample t-test**. For example, one might use a t-test to determine if exam scores for one class differ significantly from several previous sections of the same course (i.e., does the average score for the class of interest differ significantly from average scores across all other groups).

More commonly, t-tests are used to compare means between two specific groups. This is called an **independent samples t-test**. For example, when conducting an experiment where one group receives one set of instructions (e.g., focus on creating as many widgets as possible) and another group receives a different set of instructions (e.g., focus on mastering the process of creating widgets), one might use a t-test to determine which, if either, set of instructions produces the best results.

Like many other statistical techniques, t-tests produce an alpha used to determine how likely it is that any difference between groups is simply due to chance. As with correlation and regression, this alpha is impacted by both the magnitude of the effect (the size of the differences between groups) and by sample sizes. Larger effects and larger sample sizes result in lower alphas, meaning it is less likely that a difference is simply due to chance. With t-tests, the magnitude of the effect is determined by the standard difference in group means. So, it is not just the difference in average scores between the two groups that matter, but how that difference compares to the overall variance in scores for all subjects in both groups. In other words, the more spread out scores are, the lower the magnitude of the difference (and the less likely that results will be statistically significant).

Key terms:

- **Repeated measure/paired samples t-test** – Used to determine if scores differ between two groups matched on a particular characteristic. Most commonly, these are scores that come from the same subjects measured at two different points in time. So, one might assess a group's proficiency on a certain task both before and after training to determine if the training helped them improve.

- **d-scores (or difference scores)** – A standardized difference score (i.e., the raw score difference divided by the standard deviation of a measure).

Examples:

Consider exam scores from two sections of the same Introduction to Psychology course taught by two different instructors: Dr. Smith and Dr. Johnson (see the table below). We can use a t-test to determine how likely the difference between scores is simply due to chance.

Table 9.1 – Average exam scores from two different sections of the same course

Section #	Instructor	Class Size	Mean Score	Score SD
1	Dr. Smith	22	94.32	10.04
2	Dr. Johnson	21	80.90	12.36

T-test results for this example are significant ($p < .01$). Because our alpha (p) is less than .01, there is less than a 1% chance that the observed difference in scores between the two sections is due to chance. In other words, Dr. Smith's class scored significantly higher than Dr. Johnson's class.

What to Watch For:

When interpreting results from a t-test, one must be very careful to consider why any differences between groups might exist. For example, consider the results above. At face value, it would seem as though Dr. Smith is a more effective instructor because exam scores from his class are significantly higher than scores from Dr.

Johnson's class. But, what if Dr. Smith focuses more on teaching to the exam, or if his class is an honor's class where Dr. Johnson's is not? As with correlation, one must try to account for unforeseen variables (e.g., to what degree an instructor teaches to the exam or other differences between groups such as one section being an honor's class) that account for the observed effect.

Food for Thought:

The figure below shows average SAT scores from 1998. These results pertain to findings that, throughout the 1990s, average state spending per student was negatively correlated with SAT performance. As seen in the figure, average scores for North Dakota and New Jersey do seem to indicate that higher spending might actually result in lower SAT scores. Other than a direct causal relationship (i.e., North Dakota students did better because their state spent less per student), what else might account for this statistically significant difference?

Figure 9.1 – Average SAT scores from New Jersey and North Dakota in 1998.

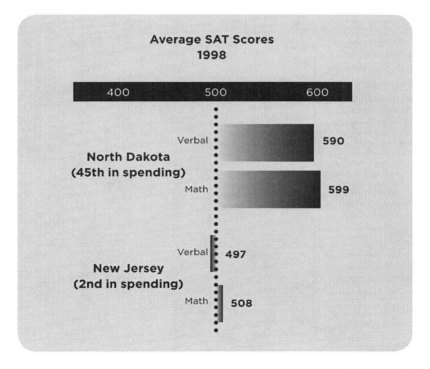

TOPIC 10 ANALYSIS OF VARIANCE (ANOVA)

Analysis of Variance (ANOVA) is similar to a t-test in many ways, but can be used to compare more than two groups to one another. A One-Way ANOVA compares multiple groups represented by only one independent variable (e.g., multiple instructors of the same course). A multivariate ANOVA compares multiple groups represented by two or more independent variables (e.g., both instructor and morning versus afternoon sections). Multivariate ANOVAs also allow for one to test interactions between multiple variables (e.g., are some instructors better at teaching morning classes whereas others are better at teaching afternoon classes?).

ANOVAs produce one or more *F-scores* and an accompanying alpha for each independent variable and each interaction. See below for an example.

Key terms:

- **Main effect** – The effect (or difference in scores) associated with each independent variable.

- **Interaction** – When the impact of one independent variable (e.g., instructor) on an outcome of interest (e.g., exam grades) is dependent on another independent variable (e.g., time of class).

- **Interaction effect** – The effect (impact on scores) of an interaction.

- **Post Hoc tests** – A set of procedures for determining if, when there is a significant main effect on a variable with more than two possible scores (e.g., three different instructors), there are differences between each potential pairing of scores (e.g., compare scores from instructor #1 and #2, #1 and #3, and #2 and #3). Common types of post hoc tests include LSD, Bonferroni, and Tukey.

- **ANCOVA** – Analysis of Covariance is similar to ANOVA but includes covariates (see Topic #8) so one can identify the effects of an independent variable on an outcome of interest after the effects of these covariates have been statistically removed.

- **MANOVA** – Multivariate Analysis of Variance is like ANOVA but with multiple outcome measures. For example, a researcher might want to determine the impact of education and parents' socioeconomic status on later career success but define success with multiple variables such as income, prestige, and job level. A significant MANOVA would indicate that, in general, both predictors impact career success (at which point the researcher would basically have to break his or her outcome variables up again and run separate ANOVAs to determine which predictors actually impact which outcomes and to what degree).

- **MANCOVA** – Like MANOVA but with the inclusion of covariates.

Examples:

To expand on the example in the previous section, consider average exam scores from six different sections of Introduction to Psychology. Three are morning classes and three are afternoon classes. There are also three different instructors. Each instructor teaches one morning and one afternoon section. Class sizes, class means, and standard deviations are presented below.

Table 10.1 – Average exam scores from six different sections of the same course.

Section #	Instructor	Time Period	Class Size	Mean Score	Score SD
1	Dr. Smith	Morning	22	94.32	10.04
2	Dr. Johnson	Morning	21	80.90	12.36
3	Dr. Jones	Morning	19	82.42	16.21
4	Dr. Smith	Afternoon	19	82.32	11.39
5	Dr. Johnson	Afternoon	20	77.95	23.07
6	Dr. Jones	Afternoon	23	92.82	7.83

In this case, the main effect for instructor is significant ($p < .01$) but the main effect for time of day is not ($p = .73$). This indicates that the instructor does have a significant impact on course performance but time of day does not. In this case, post hoc tests also indicate there is not a significant difference in average exam scores for classes taught by Drs. Smith and Jones, but average exam scores for both instructors are significantly higher than average scores for classes taught by Dr. Johnson.

With this example, there is also a significant interaction effect ($p < .01$). Interactions between two variables are usually easiest to see by graphing mean scores. As the graph below shows, Dr. Smith's morning class scored significantly higher than his afternoon class, but Dr. Jones' afternoon class scored significantly higher than her morning class. So, although we see no significant difference between scores for these two instructors when averaged across both of their sections, there is clearly a difference when time of day is taken into account.

Figure 10.1 – Average exam scores plotted on a line graph.

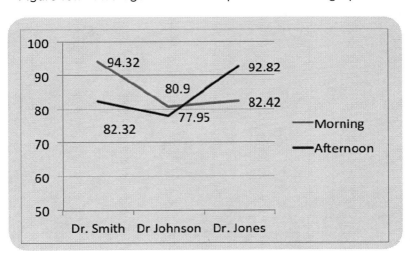

What to Watch For:

Unequal sample sizes can cause problems with ANOVAs, but there are statistical corrections that most statistical programs run automatically.

As with the previous techniques covered, one must always be aware of any unforeseen confounding variables that account for differences between groups. For example, not taking time of day into account would have potentially lead to misleading results in the example above (such as concluding that Dr. Smith's classes always outperformed Dr. Johnson's classes when, in fact, this is only true for the morning section).

Food for Thought:

Consider an example where a researcher wants to study how various components of meeting someone for the first time influences that person's impression of the researcher. The researcher uses a simple 2x2 design, meaning there are two independent variables comprised of two groups each. Those groups are 1) physical proximity – close versus distanced, and 2) topic of conversation – ask about the other person versus talking about him or herself. Overall impression is measured using a 0 (very poor) to 5 (exceptional) rating scale. Results are presented below.

Figure 10.2 – Average impression ratings plotted on a line graph.

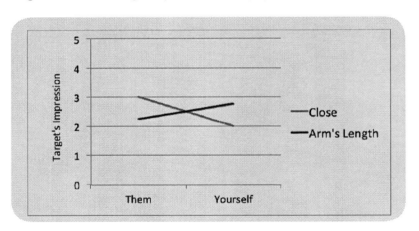

This is an example of a "crossover" or "disordinal" interaction (i.e., the lines cross when graphed this way). Such an interaction represents a pattern of results where the relationship between one independent variable and an outcome of interest clearly depends on the other independent variable. In this case, if another researcher were to repeat the study above but only look at one independent variable at a time, how would that impact his or her results?

TOPIC 11 CHI-SQUARE

Unlike the analyses covered in earlier sections of this chapter, which typically involve comparing quantitative/continuous scores (i.e., ordinal, interval, or ratio scales), Chi-square is an analytical technique used to compare scores measured using qualitative/categorical scores (i.e., nominal scales).

Chi-squares (χ^2) may be used to compare results on one variable to a predetermined set of expectations. This use of Chi-square is typically called a **goodness of fit** test. Chi-squares may also be used to determine if group membership across multiple variables is equally distributed or adheres to some other pre-determined pattern. As with the techniques covered in previous sections of this guide, a Chi-square analysis produces an alpha score that indicates how likely any deviation in results (compared to expected results) is simply due to chance.

Key terms:

- **Expected frequencies** – How subjects are expected to be divided out by groups according to some null hypothesis (e.g., could be equal across groups or any other predetermined distribution).

- **Observed frequencies** – How subjects or occurrences actually do divide out across groups.

Examples:

For an example of using Chi-square to compare results on a variable to a predetermined outcome, consider a scenario where a researcher wants to know if a die is loaded. To examine this possibility, he or she could roll the die 60 times and would generally expect each possible outcome (1-6) to occur about 10 times if the die is not loaded. One should not, however, expect each outcome to occur exactly 10 times due to random chance. Therefore, a Chi-square can help determine how likely it is that results differ from 10 equal rolls for each outcome simply due to chance.

Outcome	1	2	3	4	5	6
# of occurrences	10	12	11	7	8	12

Given the example above, the resulting Chi-square is not significant (p = .82). So, even though each possible outcome did not come up an equal number of times, it is likely this deviation is simply due to chance.

Now consider an example where a researcher wants to compare applicant interview scores (designated as pass/fail) to performance on an assessment center (also designated as pass/fail). If the two are unrelated, one would expect the same pass/fail ratio on the assessment center for those passing the interview and those not passing the interview.

	Failed Assessment Center	Passed Assessment Center	Percent Passing Assessment Center
Failed Interview	29	16	36%
Passed Interview	21	34	62%

The resulting Chi-square is significant (p = .02), which indicates the two are likely related. In other words, those passing the interview are also more likely to pass the assessment center. But how likely one might ask? To answer this question, one can simply calculate (a) the percentage of people passing the assessment center who failed the interview and (b) the percentage passing the assessment center who passed the interview. For those failing the interview, 16 out of 45 passed the assessment center (36%). For those passing the interview, 34 out of 55 passed the assessment center (62%). In other words, people who pass the interview are almost twice as likely to also pass the assessment center (compared to those who do not pass the interview).

Granted, given that interviews and assessment centers commonly produce continuous rather than categorical scores, one could also use a correlation to examine the association between these two variables. But, saying that two scores are correlated at a certain level (e.g., likely around .30 for the example above) is often not as clear and direct as using something like the 2x2 table presented above.

What to Watch For:

Chi-square often is, but usually shouldn't be, used when there are low base rates for any one group on either variable. **Low base rates** are the result of very few people falling within any particular group. This not only causes problems for the calculation of the statistic itself, but can lead to very misleading results.

For example, in most jobs serious accidents and injuries do happen, but they are rare. Consider a study examining the impact of safety training on serious accidents and injuries, which only occur approximately 1% of the time. Results are as follows:

	No Major Accidents or Injuries	Had a Major Accident or Injury	Percent with a major Accident or Injury
No Training	208	5	2.35%
Received Training	386	1	0.26%

With these results, there is a significant Chi-square (Đ = .02) and an examination of the percentage of those with accidents shows that individuals who did not receive training are over nine times more likely to have a serious accident or injury than those who did receive training. Granted, these are impressive results and certainly indicate the training likely had some impact, or at least more likely than what one would expect due to chance. But, what if the research finds that a handful of people received training but were originally categorized as "No Training?" If that were true for just one person who had an accident (so now 4 people with injuries didn't receive training and 2 people with injuries did receive training), the Chi-square would no longer be significant (Đ = .19). In this case, those without training would only be about three times more likely to have had an accident or injury than those who received training. This would still indicate that training may have had some impact, but the results now look very different based on just one person in a sample of 600. Now change data for just two people out of 600 and it would appear as though the training had little to no impact.

Food for Thought:

Chi-square results might be biased when potential influential or confounding variables are ignored. One notorious example comes from a review of Berkeley admissions by gender based on data collected in 1973. The first table below shows the overall admission rates by gender, which because of the large sample sizes, results in a statistically significant bias towards males.

	Applicants	Admitted
Men	8442	44%
Women	4321	35%

But, when broken down by department, the analysis shows a slight (but statistically significant) bias towards females.

Department	Men		Women	
	Applicants	Admitted	Applicants	Admitted
A	825	62%	108	82%
B	560	63%	25	68%
C	325	37%	593	34%
D	417	33%	375	35%
E	191	28%	393	24%
F	272	6%	341	7%

How is this possible?

Chapter 3

STATISTICAL TECHNIQUES #3 — MORE COMPLEX STUFF

Several of the topics covered in this chapter involve more complex statistical procedures that are often covered in graduate level statistics courses. Covering them in detail can frequently involve entire courses dedicated to their review. The one exception is the first topic of this chapter, Exploratory Factor Analysis (Topic #12), which can be conducted fairly quickly and easily in SPSS or SAS. Still, even that is a topic that requires a lot of training and experience to perform properly.

In addition, running analyses for the remaining topics covered in this chapter not only require specialized knowledge, but specialized software programs. In other words, by far the best way to conduct many of these analyses is by finding someone who is trained and up-to-date on the topic and asking that person for help. Still, the information in the following topic areas offers a review of concepts and terms to help you understand the basics.

TOPIC 12 EXPLORATORY FACTOR ANALYSIS

Exploratory factor analysis (EFA) involves a variety of methods aimed at helping build scales from the ground up. The basic idea behind EFA is to evaluate a large number of responses on multiple items to see which ones "hang together," which is just a phrase to indicate that items measure the same general construct. This is indicated by the fact they tend to correlate highly with one another.

Factors are linear combinations of items that are similar to predicted outcome variables produced from regression (see Topic #8). In other words, factors represent the best way to add scores on individual items to represent the factor or construct of interest. Most programs for conducting EFAs allow for factor scores to be saved as new variables. These new variables represent each subject's estimated score on a given factor based on their scores from the items that comprise that factor. A researcher can then use scores on this new variable like any other variable in subsequent analyses. For example, there is no perfect measure of IQ. But, if a researcher gives 100 subjects three different IQ tests, results could be combined to create a "factor" score based on a subject's results from all three tests. Because this factor score is calculated using results from a larger and more varied set of items, it is likely a more accurate representation of true IQ than results from any one individual IQ test.

EFA is not only useful for creating new scales, but also for evaluating the structure of existing assessments that contain multiple scales. If an assessment claims to measure multiple scales, an EFA should be able to confirm that each individual item loads onto the correct scale or factor.

Technically, EFA provides information on as many possible factors as there are items in the analysis. The question one needs to answer when running an EFA is how many important factors actually exist. In other words, based on EFA results, a researcher must determine how many factors to "retain" or keep in a final solution. Also, each item receives a loading on each factor.

In general, this is similar to a correlation between the item and the factor. Factor loadings for items typically need to be at least .30 or .40 to conclude that the item "loads" onto the factor.

To help identify which factors are the most important, each factor receives an eigenvalue. **Eigenvalues** represent the amount of variance accounted for by that factor. When a factor represents a lot of items that are highly correlated with one another, it will have a high eigenvalue. Eigenvalues are actually a ratio, so 1.00 is a critical value. Although having an eigenvalue of 1.00 or greater does not necessarily mean that factor is important, rarely if ever is there justification for retaining a factor with an eigenvlaue of less than 1.00.

Unfortunately, determining the number of factors to retain from an EFA isn't an exact science. Instead, it often involves running analyses over and over again by examining different items and numbers of factors to retain. When several items load onto a factor, and an inspection of the items indicates they clearly measure the same general construct, one should usually keep them. When items don't load onto any factor or load onto too many factors, one often wants to remove them and then rerun the factor analysis. The process of finding a good solution that makes sense can easily involve dozens of factor analyses.

Key terms:

- **Principle Component Analysis (PCA)** – A method related to, but not entirely identical to, EFA. Often, when someone performs a PCA, they call it a factor analysis and results are typically reported and interpreted the same way.

- **Scree plot** – A plot of eigenvalues from largest to smallest. Often (and hopefully) there is a place in this plot where values clearly drop significantly and then level out around or just below 1.00. When this is the case, the best solution is often the one that retains all factors before that sudden drop.

- **Orthogonal solutions** – Methods that report results for factors that are not correlated with one another.

- **Oblique solutions** – Methods that allow factors to be correlated with one another.

- **Rotations** – methods for statistically manipulating factor analysis results so solutions are easier to interpret. When performing a factor analysis using an orthogonal solution, it is often necessary to perform a rotation to render results easier to interpret.

- **Cross-loadings** – When an individual item loads heavily on two or more scales. Items with high cross loadings can either be dropped from an assessment or simply used in the calculation of more than one scale (although that will result in each scale being more highly correlated with one another than they otherwise would have been).

Examples:

Below is an example of PCA results (with Varimax rotation) for 10 cognitive ability items. Figure 12.1 displays eigenvalues for each of the 10 potential factors (again, there are 10 factors because there are 10 items). As seen in these results, three factors have eigenvalues of 1.00 or greater, although there is clearly a drop off after the first factor. This drop off indicates that a one factor solution likely best fits these data. Next are the rotated factor loadings for the three factor solution (originally reported in SPSS because the default is to retain all factors with eigenvalues of 1.00 or higher) and a one factor solution (created after specifying results for just a one factor solution in SPSS.

Figure 12.1 – Scree plot for 10 cognitive ability items

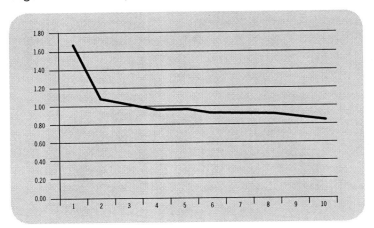

Table 12.1 – Factor analysis results for 10 cognitive ability items

Factor	Eigenvalue	Item #	Factor 1	Factor 2	Factor 3	Item #	Factor 1
1	1.71	1	-0.05	0.50	0.36	1	0.38
2	1.07	2	0.07	0.02	0.86	2	0.22
3	1.00	3	-0.01	0.63	-0.11	3	0.41
4	0.94	4	0.52	-0.02	0.21	4	0.39
5	0.93	5	0.46	0.14	-0.06	5	0.41
6	0.90	6	0.49	0.22	-0.24	6	0.45
7	0.89	7	0.15	0.64	-0.07	7	0.53
8	0.88	8	0.49	0.08	0.14	8	0.42
9	0.86	9	0.16	0.48	0.14	9	0.47
10	0.82	10	0.60	-0.04	-0.05	10	0.38

In the three factor solution, five items load strongly on the first factor, four on the second factor, and only one on the third factor. In the one factor solution, all but one item (#2) has a factor loading of at least .30 on the factor, but only six items have factor loadings of at least .40 or higher. So, this set of items generally hangs together fairly well, but one could probably improve it with some replacement items. For example, replacing the four items with loadings of less than .40 with four new items (selected after running several alternatives), an EFA produces the following results:

Figure 12.2 – Scree plot for alternative item set

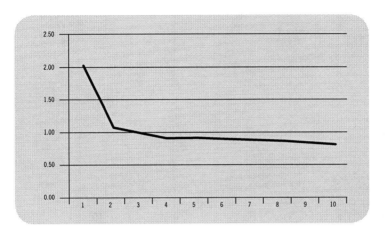

Table 12.2 – Results for alternative item set

Factor	Eigenvalue	Item #	Factor 1
1	2.07	12	0.43
2	1.07	15	0.56
3	0.94	3	0.39
4	0.91	17	0.42
5	0.90	5	0.36
6	0.87	6	0.56
7	0.86	7	0.54
8	0.84	8	0.35
9	0.79	9	0.44
10	0.75	18	0.54

As shown in these results, there is even stronger evidence of a one factor solution (with an eigenvalue greater than 2.00 and a larger drop off between the first and second factor). Assuming the intent is to develop one 10 item scale that represents only one factor, this second set of items works better than the first. But notice that factor loadings for some of the initial items have now dropped to less than .40. To continue to improve the scale, the next step would involve examining additional potential replacement items to see if any from the current set can be replaced with items that have higher factor loadings.

As demonstrated by this example, the process of identifying the best possible set of items to create a one-factor scale can be not only time consuming, but requires data from a large number of possible items.

What to Watch For:

Several characteristics of one's sample and items can impact the results of an EFA. The first is how highly correlated items on each scale are with one another. The stronger the relationship between the items on each scale, the stronger the overall factor analysis results will be. The opposite, however, can be true when scales are highly correlated with one another. When scales are correlated, individual items often have higher cross loadings, which can make everything messier.

Anytime anyone presents EFA results, it is important to ask if they examined alternative solutions. For example, just because someone finds a good three factor solution that makes sense to them (and even you), it doesn't mean a four factor solution might not have worked better.

Another important consideration is the examination of positively versus negatively scored items. For example, if measuring how outgoing a person is, one might write two very similar but oppositely scored items: "I enjoy talking to others" and "I do not enjoy interacting with others." Many scales do and should include both positively and negatively oriented items. But, when such items load on the same factor, one will have a positive loading and the other will have a negative loading. Furthermore, the "positively" worded items might have negative loadings and the "negatively" worded items might have positive loadings. The direction of the individual item loadings doesn't really matter, but it often is beneficial to include both types of items.

Also, EFA requires large samples to run properly. Although there is some debate concerning how large samples must be, two general rules of thumb are that they need to be (a) at least 100 and (b) at least five times greater than the number of items. In other words, the more items a researcher has, the more subjects required to run a factor analysis.

Finally, dozens of different methods and approaches exist for running EFAs. The most common (even though it is technically not a factor analysis) is a Principal Components Analysis (PCA) with Varimax rotation. Often, results are very similar regardless of the method, but it is important to try different methods. If nothing else, this helps confirm that results are consistent regardless of method.

Food for Thought:

Consider the results below concerning a factor analysis conducted on six items designed to measure how quickly a person makes decisions. The items are:

1. I like to do things on the spur of the moment.

2. I frequently do things on impulse.

3. Life is no fun when you play it safe.

4. I don't like work that requires close attention to details.

5. I prefer to watch the "big picture" and leave details to others.

6. I tend to get bored with details.

Based on data collected from 1,000 individuals who responded to these items, EFA results are as follows:

Table 12.3 – EFA results for example items

Factor	Eigenvalue	Item #	Factor 1	Item #	Factor 1	Factor 2
1	2.29	1	0.53	1	0.53	0.68
2	1.67	2	0.58	2	0.58	0.60
3	0.73	3	0.49	3	0.49	0.58
4	0.53	4	0.62	4	0.62	-0.49
5	0.40	5	0.70	5	0.70	-0.44
6	0.38	6	0.75	6	0.75	-0.42

These results present somewhat of a dilemma in that one could argue for either a one or two factor solution. Based on the factor loadings for both options, which solution is better?

TOPIC 13 STRUCTURAL EQUATION MODELING

Structural Equation Modeling (SEM) is a method for examining complex relationships across multiple variables. In a sense, SEM allows someone to draw a picture of what they think relationships between variables should look like and then examine how well that picture represents the actual relationships among variables in their data. The picture itself represents the relationships between variables (e.g., which variables are associated with one another and which variables are not). This predefined set of relationships between variables represents the model that a person tests with SEM.

SEM models may be comprised of both variables (represented as squares or rectangles) and factors (represented as circles or ovals – see Topic #12 for a discussion of factors). Models that contain only variables are generally analyzed the same way as other SEMs, but the procedure is called a **Path Analysis**.

Unlike many other types of analyses, there is not one specific result to interpret with SEM. Instead, SEM produces a number of results, most of which are known as fit indices. These **fit indices** represent different methods for examining how well a model accurately represents the full set of relationships between variables in a dataset.

Confirmatory Factor Analysis (CFA) is similar to an EFA (Topic #12) in that it is a method for determining how well items load onto specific factors. But with CFA, a person uses SEM techniques to first define which items he or she expects to load onto each factor. This represents the "model" tested using SEM. Below are examples of CFA models for the 1-factor and 2-factor solutions presented at the end of Topic #12.

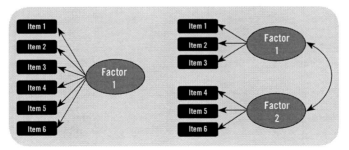

Key terms:

- **Exogenous variables** – Similar to an independent variable, an exogenous variable is any variable in an SEM that isn't being predicted (i.e., has no arrows pointing towards it) by any other variable.

- **Endogenous variables** – Similar to a dependent variable, an endogenous variable is any variable that is being predicted (i.e., has at least one arrow pointing towards it) by another variable. One might also use endogenous variables to predict other variables in subsequent stages in a model (see the example below).

- **Parameters** – Each possible relationship between every variable in a model. In other words, every single variable included in a model might or might not have a relationship with every other variable. That relationship between each pair of variables (or lack thereof) is called a parameter.

- **Constrained/Fixed parameters** – Relationships between variables that are set to a specific value. For example, when a model does not specify that two variables should be related (i.e., there is no arrow connecting the two), the parameter reflecting their relationship is constrained to, or predicted to be, 0.00.

- **Free parameters** – Parameters that are allowed to fluctuate in a model. Usually, this means that, when a researcher expects variables to be related to one another, they draw a line connecting the two variables and then evaluate SEM results to determine what that relationship (if any) exists.

- **Error terms** – For the most part, all endogenous variables must have an error term associated with them. This term represents the variance in the variable that is not accurately predicted by other variables in the model. Even though error terms are essential for a model to run properly, they are often not included in graphical representations of a model.

- **Common Fit Indices:**

    - **Chi-square** – The statistical result of a Chi-square in SEM is basically the same thing as the goodness of fit Chi-

Square (see Topic #11). With SEM, Chi-Square represents goodness of fit for an entire SEM model, or, how well the relationships in a dataset fit with the expectations outlined in the model. Unfortunately, with large enough samples, Chi-square is almost always significant. Although this means the data do not fit the model, it is an overly conservative estimate with large sample sizes. In such cases, other fit indices are usually given more credence when interpreting SEM model fit.

- **Comparative Fit Index (CFI)** – CFI depends, in large part, on the strength of relationships between variables associated with one another in a model. In general, a CFI of .90 or higher is considered reasonable or a good fit.

- **Root Mean Square Error of Approximation (RMSEA)** – Because it is based on how much proposed relationships in a model deviate from actual relationships in one's data, lower RMSEA values indicate better model fit. Generally, a RMSEA of .05 or less is considered good fit while .10 or higher indicates a poor fit.

- **Standardized Root Mean Residual (SRMR)** – Similar to RMSEA, lower values for SRMR indicate better model fit. Again, a SRMR smaller than .05 is generally considered an indication of a good fit.

- **Model modification** – When a researcher makes changes to their model (either adding in new relationships between model components or removing unnecessary components) to improve model fit. The two primary statistical techniques (called **modification indices**) for identifying potentially useful model modifications are:

  - **Wald Test** – Indicates how much model fit would improve if a path were removed from a model.

  - **Lagrange Multiplier** – Indicates how much model fit would improve if a path were added to a model.

Examples:

Below is an example of an SEM showing relationships between six personality-based safety scales, safety-related job performance (measured using supervisory performance ratings of safety-related behaviors), and safety outcomes (measured using organizational records of injuries and accidents across at least a three year period). The first figure represents the initial model tested for these analyses, which proposes that each of the six personality-based safety scales predict safety performance, which in turn, predicts safety outcomes. The second figure is the final model after reviewing results concerning model fit and modification indices. The numbers in the second figure represent relationships between variables (similar to correlation coefficients). Those that are significant at an alpha level of < .05 are marked with an "*".

Figure 13.1 – Initial model to be tested

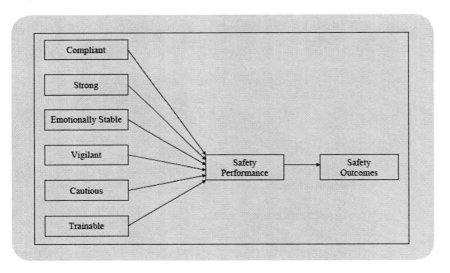

Figure 13.2 – Final model with results for each path

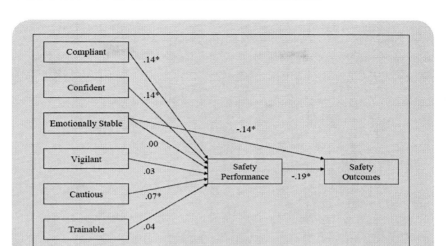

As shown in the second figure, three of the six personality-based safety scales significantly predict safety performance. Furthermore, safety performance significantly predicts safety outcomes (which is a negative relationship because higher safety-related performance ratings predicted fewer accidents and injuries). However, notice the addition of a direct link between Emotionally Stable and safety outcomes, indicating that adding this link significantly improved model fit. In other words, although Emotionally Stable was not a direct predictor of Safety Performance ratings, it was directly related to safety outcomes.

What to Watch For:

As with EFA (Topic #12), there is no agreed upon rule for how large sample sizes need to be to run an SEM, but they do need to be large. In general, one needs at least 200 to 400 subjects to consider running an SEM. In addition, more subjects are required when a model contains more variables. A general rule of thumb is that SEM requires least 10 to 20 subjects for each variable in a model.

Also, just because a model fits a set of data well does not mean it is the best possible model. As with EFA, SEM often requires that one test many different models before reaching the best solution. However, individuals using SEM should avoid making changes to their model simply based on results from modification indices. To do so would run the risk of what is called "over-fitting" data, meaning making changes to a model based simply on sampling error. In other words, if adding or removing some paths do not make sense, it is usually best to leave them alone. Therefore, when reviewing SEM results, it is important to compare the initial predicted model to the final outcome and question any modifications that have been made to improve fit.

Food for Thought:

As we've stated, SEM essentially involves drawing a picture to indicate which variables of interest in a dataset relate to one another and which ones do not. Granted, this is an overly simplistic portrayal of SEM, but it still provides a basic idea of what SEM generally does in practice.

Because each potential "relationship" is represented by the correlation between any two variables included in a model, the number of potential relationships grows exponentially as the number of variables grow (e.g., two variables can only be correlated with one another, three variables provides three potential variable pairs, four provides six potential variable pairs, five provides ten potential variable pairs, and so on).

What are the potential implications of running an SEM using more and more variables in one's model?

TOPIC 14 META-ANALYSIS

Meta-analysis is a term that refers to any process used to combine results across multiple samples and/or studies. In other words, meta-analytical procedures provide a way to combine results across studies intended to investigate the same general effect (i.e., associations between similar variables or differences between similar groups on one or more outcomes of interest).

In I/O Psychology, the term meta-analysis usually refers to a more specific set of procedures used to combine effects across studies. These effects are usually correlations between two variables (although the same general principles apply when using differences between groups, represented by d-scores as outlined in Topic #9). Meta-analysis began to gain popularity within I/O Psychology in the 1980's. Prior to this time, researchers examining the same relationships would often find different results and interpret these differences as indications that the studies themselves differed in important ways (e.g., different measures, jobs, organizations). However, even when studies are similar in every way conceivable, results often vary across samples simply due to sampling error. This is especially true for studies with small samples, in which the impact of sampling error is greatest.

Meta-analysis, therefore, is similar to performing a study by using subjects from all previous studies that have already examined the topic of interest. For example, if five different researchers examined the relationship between cognitive ability and job performance and found correlations varying anywhere from .05 to .35, researchers might attribute these differences to samples, jobs, organizations, industries, or any of hundreds of other differences that might exist between studies. By combining effects across studies, however, the result is an estimate of the relationship between cognitive ability and job performance across all studies examined (e.g., .20). To help account for sampling error, meta-analysis procedures give studies with larger sample sizes more weight than studies with smaller sample sizes. Also, most meta-analysis procedures provide an estimate of how much of the variation across studies can be attributed to sampling error. In other words, after controlling for sampling error, are there still differences across studies that are producing different results.

Meta-analysis has two primary advantages. First, because meta-analysis relies on results from multiple studies, sample sizes are much larger than one could ever get from any single study. This helps account for sampling error. Second, meta-analysis allows one to correct for statistical artifacts, which are problems with samples or data that may impact results. In other words, statistical artifacts are factors that introduce error into measures. One artifact is sampling error, but others include range restriction and a lack of reliability (see Topics #5 and #7). Meta-analysis provides methods for statistically correcting or controlling for each of these sources of error, which produces an estimate of what a relationship might be if these errors did not exist. For example, even though it is impossible to measure anything with perfect precision, especially when collecting data from human subjects, meta-analytical corrections help estimate what results would be if perfect measures were possible. This is done by mathematically estimating how artifacts, such as range restriction or a lack of perfect reliability, generally lower the correlation between two variables and then estimating what the correlation would be if those artifacts did not exist.

Key terms:

- **k** – The symbol used to represent the number of studies included in a meta-analysis.

- **N** – The symbol used to represent the total number of cases or subjects across all studies.

- **Observed validity or observed effect size** – usually reported as r_{obs}, this result represents the observed correlation after taking sampling error into account. In other words, it is the sample weighted average (where smaller samples receive less consideration than larger samples) of the effect examined across all studies. A meta-analysis which reports only observed scores (i.e., not corrected for any other statistical artifacts other than sampling error), is often called a **bare bones meta-analysis**.

- **Operational validity/effect size** – When one corrects results for only range restriction in a predictor measure and unreliability in an outcome measure. This is often used to examine relationships between potential selection measures (e.g., cognitive ability, personality, interview scores, assessment center results) and job performance, if job performance could be measured with perfect reliability.

- **True validity/effect size** – When one corrects for everything he or she can, including unreliability in predictor measures. The idea is to estimate what the relationship would be between a predictor measure and an outcome measure if both could be measured with perfect reliability. For example, even though one might never be able to measure cognitive ability with 100% accuracy, true validity provides an estimate of how much cognitive ability influences job performance in the real world if both could be measured with perfect reliability.

- **Confidence Interval** – Used in meta-analysis primarily as a method for evaluating the statistical significance of one's results. A 95% confidence interval provides similar information to what one gets from a p-value or alpha from many other common statistical techniques. That is because a 95% confidence interval that does not include 0.00 means two variables are significantly correlated with one another at a .05 alpha level. Anytime one has an alpha, it is usually possible to also produce a confidence interval around one's effect, but the practice is currently most common with meta-analyses.

- **Percentage of variance accounted for by artifacts** – Most meta-analyses report an estimate of the percentage of variance accounted for across results from different studies due to artifacts. When this result is 100%, there is no evidence that other variables contribute to differences in findings across studies other than artifacts. In other words, results are consistent across samples even though observed correlations within each study are not exactly equal (i.e., all differences can be attributed to sampling error).

- **Moderators** – When less than 100% of the variance in study results can be attributed to statistical artifacts, other factors might contribute to differences in results across individual studies. These factors are moderators, in that they are outside variables that influence the relationship between two other variables. For example, results have shown that cognitive ability is likely more predictive of performance for complex jobs compared to less complex jobs. Job complexity, therefore, moderates the relationship between cognitive ability and job performance because that relationship is higher in magnitude for highly complex jobs but lower in magnitude for less complex jobs.

- **Credibility Interval** – When there is evidence of potential moderators (i.e., the percentage of variance in study results accounted for by artifacts is less than 100%), credibility intervals indicate how much an effect size is likely to fluctuate across all possible samples. For example, given that job complexity likely moderates the relationship between cognitive ability and job performance, that relationship will not be the same across all jobs. An 80% credibility interval of .25 - .35 would mean that, although the relationship is not the same for all jobs, the correlation falls somewhere between .25 and .35 for 80% of all jobs.

Examples:

Meta-analyses are particularly popular in the world of I/O Psychology for examining relationships between measures used to predict performance and job performance ratings. Below are results from meta-analyses for some of the most commonly used selection measures.

Table 14.1 Comparative Validity of Assessments for Predicting Overall Job Performance

Study	Predictor	r_{obs}
A.	Conscientiousness Tests	.18
B.	Integrity Tests	.21
C.	Structured Interviews	.18
D.	Unstructured Interviews	.11
E.	Situational Judgment Tests	.20
F.	Biodata	.22
G.	General Mental Ability	.21
H.	Assessment Centers	.28
I.	Resumes	.18

Note. r_{obs} = mean observed validity; A = Mount & Barrick (2001). B = Ones, Viswesvaran, & Schmidt (1993). C & D = McDaniel, Whetzel, Schmidt, & Maurer (1994). E = McDaniel, Hartman, Whetzel, & Grubb (2007). F = Bliesener (1996). G = Pearlman, Schmidt, & Hunter (1980). H = Arthur et al. (2003). I = O'Leary (2009).

Also, hundreds of studies prior to the 1990's examined the relationship between different personality variables and job performance. Two of the most widely referenced studies in I/O Psychology (one by Barrick & Mount and one by Tett, Jackson, and Rothstein – both published in 1991) were meta-analyses that combined results across many of these earlier studies. In general, both showed that differences in previous individual studies were largely the result of sampling error. For example, regardless of results from individual studies, these meta-analyses showed that Conscientiousness (i.e., being hard working and detail oriented) significantly predicted job performance across a range of jobs, organizations, and industries.

Furthermore, researchers can use meta-analysis to investigate moderators of relationships between variables. For example, the Barrick and Mount meta-analysis published in 1991, as well as several that have been published since, show that Extraversion (i.e., being outgoing and sociable) is predictive of performance for managers and sales employees but not employees in many other job categories (e.g., skilled and semi-skilled workers).

What to Watch For:

One of the biggest concerns with many meta-analyses is what is commonly called the **file drawer problem**. This term refers to the fact that, because it is often difficult to get results published if one's results are not statistically significant, non-significant results are not widely available to researchers interested in a certain topic (i.e., they just get locked away in some researcher's file drawer forever). As a result, if all a researcher has available are results that have been published, it is likely he or she will miss results from studies that found smaller, non-significant effects. There are some statistical methods one can use to try to account for the file drawer problem, but the most common approach is to simply reach out to researchers who have studied the same area and ask if they have any unpublished results they can share. One should review any meta-analysis that does not include an explanation of efforts to account for the file drawer problem with some skepticism.

Also, there continues to be debate concerning the ability of meta-analysis to reveal potential moderators, or unknown variables that might influence the relationships between variables. If the samples used in a meta-analysis are not representative of the entire population of interest, potential moderators might go unnoticed. For example, if a meta-analysis examines the relationships between measures of work-family conflict and job satisfaction but is based primarily on samples from entry level employees, the percentage of variance accounted for in results might be 100%. That does not mean, however, that the results accurately reflect the relationship between work-family conflict and job satisfaction for other samples such as managers and business owners.

Food for Thought:

As cited above, the relationship between Conscientiousness and job performance was not only well documented in the early 1990's, but in numerous meta-analyses since that time. However, a handful of recent meta-analyses have also examined the correlations between various measures of Conscientiousness that were often grouped together in these earlier studies. These results, which reflect the degree to which different Conscientiousness scales correlate with one another, have been disappointing to many proponents of personality testing (e.g., often lower than .50). This brings into question how well all of these different "Conscientiousness" measures actually measure the same thing. What are some of the potential implications of these recent results?

TOPIC 15 MEDIATION & MODERATION

Mediation versus Moderation is probably one of the most common Comprehensive Exam topics in all of I/O Psychology graduate programs, likely because it is often a cause of confusion for even the most statistically savvy I/O types. The source for this confusion is fairly easy to see. First, both deal with a third variable somehow influencing the relationship between two other variables. Second, they sound a lot alike, which probably just adds to the confusion.

With **mediation**, the impact of one variable on another operates through a third variable. So, if researchers only examine the relationship between their predictor variables and their outcome variables of interest, they will find a relationship. But, they are failing to see the entire picture if they don't also take into account that this relationship exists because of a third variable (their mediating variable) that fits in between the two. Mediation can be tested through either regression or SEM.

The most common form of testing mediation is through regression (see Topic #7), which involves three steps. First, the predictor variable and outcome variable must be significantly related to one another. Second, the predictor variable and mediating variable must be significantly related to one another. Finally, when including both the predictor and mediating variable in a regression equation used to predict the outcome variable, the predictor variable is no longer as predictive. In other words, the mediating variable now becomes the most important or strongest predictor of the two.

With **moderation**, a third variable changes the relationship between two other variables. In other words, the relationship between two variables depends on scores from a third variable. In essence, moderation is simply an interaction (see Topic #10). As such, the most common way to examine potential moderating variables is to determine if interaction effects are significant.

Key terms:

- **Full mediation** – When 100% of the association between two variables is due to the mediation effects of a third variable.

- **Partial mediation** – When some but not all of the association between two variables is due to the mediation effects of a third variable.

Examples:

Mediation occurs all of the time in the real world. For example, consider how the individual characteristics of specific employees ultimately impact an organization's performance. If an organization consistently hires talented and motivated employees, it is likely to do better. But, this relationship is mediated by job behaviors. Simply hiring a bunch of talented and motivated people and putting them in an empty room does not necessarily benefit a company. But, when applied to job-related tasks, these individual characteristics influence job-related behaviors, which in turn, influence an organization's overall bottom line. In other words, job behaviors mediate the relationship between individual employee characteristics and organizational performance.

Moderation is also quite common, but often hard to detect in research because one must first know what potential moderator variables to look for and then have large samples to statistically detect potential interactions. For example, research has repeatedly shown that the impact of training on future job performance is moderated by the opportunity to engage in activities covered during the training. Although no training will result in no job performance improvements, training only influences job performance if employees are given the opportunity to use what they learned.

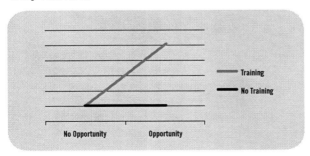

What to Watch For:

The biggest concern with both mediation and moderation is simply not being able to foresee and, therefore, know to collect data on relevant mediating or moderating variables. The failure to measure and account for a mediating variable usually just means a researcher will fail to see the "big picture", because he or she has failed to include important variables. Missing moderators, however, can be more problematic because failing to take an important moderator into account may result in failing to see differences that actually exist.

For example, refer back to the example provided under Topic #10 (ANOVA). There was a significant interaction in that Dr. Smith's morning class performed much better than his afternoon class whereas Dr. Jones's afternoon class performed much better than her morning class. In this case, time of day is a significant and meaningful moderator variable. Failing to realize this (e.g., perhaps only collecting data during morning classes without realizing that time of day might matter) could lead one to reach drastically different conclusions than if one were to collect data during only afternoon classes.

Food for Thought:

To make the distinction between mediation and moderation even more confusing, the same variable can act as both depending on the other variables one includes in his or her research. For example, safety climate (i.e., the degree to which safe working behaviors are both possible and encouraged in a work environment) has been found to both mediate and moderate relationships between other variables. Can you think of a way safety climate could be a mediator? How about a moderator?

TOPIC 16 BASICS OF ITEM RESPONSE THEORY (IRT)

Classical Test Theory (CTT) is a general designation for a wide variety of analyses that have dominated I/O psychology since the turn of the 20th Century. These analyses concern test construction and evaluation, and use many of the techniques (e.g., reliability, validity) described in early sections of this guide.

More recently, however, many I/O psychologists have begun using Item Response Theory (IRT) for assessment construction and evaluation. Because IRT analyses require a good amount of computer horsepower to run, advancements in IT capabilities in the 1990's started to make IRT more widely available to test publishers. It is now a necessary component for most commercial assessments that are adaptive (see below) or employ parallel forms (see Topic #5).

IRT involves a variety of analyses that provide more in-depth item and scale information than what CTT approaches typically provide. The fundamental premise behind IRT involves identifying the information provided by specific items at all potential points on a scale. For example, very easy math problems provide the most information at the low end of a scale that measures math ability because they distinguish only those individuals with low ability from those with everyone else. This is because individuals with average or higher ability inevitably get "easy" items correct. In contrast, very difficult math problems provide the most information at the high end of a scale because individuals without a high level of math ability are very unlikely to get these items correct. In other words, difficult items only distinguish very high ability individuals from everyone else.

The aim of IRT is to construct scales using items that provide the most possible information at ranges of interest on a scale. When trying to cover all possible ability levels, a scale must include a variety of easy, moderate, and difficult items. In contrast, when only trying to distinguish the very best from everyone else, a scale may include only difficult items.

Traditionally, IRT has predominantly been used for the construction of standardized tests in the educational arena. It is particularly useful when items have clear right and wrong answers and when publishers must construct new tests on a regular basis. For example, most standardized college admission exams, such as the GRE and GMAT, rely heavily on IRT because, not only do their items have clearly recognizable correct answers, but new versions of the tests must be created each year.

One critical assumption of most commonly used IRT models is that a scale is designed to measure a single underlying trait, designated with theta (Θ). The objective is to construct items that pinpoint a person's true score on theta, which represents their true ability level on the construct measured by the scale (e.g., math ability). There are other IRT models for dealing with multi-dimensional scales (see Topic #5), but the most common models deal with unidimensional scales, or those intended to measure only one construct.

The three most common IRT models are designated by the number of parameters, or different pieces of information, they provide for each item. For example, the simplest model is the 1 parameter model (1PL – also commonly known as the **Rasch Model**). With the 1PL model, the primary piece of information of interest is item difficulty, denoted with b. Information on each item can be used, therefore, to rank order items in terms of difficulty. Technically, the Rasch Model is a specific kind of 1PL model, but the two terms are often used interchangeably.

The two-parameter model (2PL) adds a second piece of information, known as the discrimination factor. This factor helps identify at what points on theta an item provides the most information. For example, two items might have the same overall difficulty (e.g., 50% of all respondents tend to get the item correct), but one provides information across a large ability range, because the chances of getting the item correct gradually increases as ability increases, whereas the other provides information across a short ability range, because people below a certain level are very unlikely to get the item correct but those with slightly higher ability are suddenly very likely to get it correct.

Finally, the three parameter model (3PL) includes a guessing factor. In other words, it takes into account the likelihood that someone low on ability will get an item correct simply by guessing the correct answer. This is particularly useful with multiple choice items where even random responses might result in a 20% or 25% correct response rate.

Key terms:

- **Computer Adaptive Tests (CAT)** – A method for providing test takers with the fewest possible items that target their ability level. Often based on IRT results, test publishers can develop systems for presenting items to individuals that gradually pinpoint their ability range. For example, if a person gets a couple of easy items correct, there is no need to continue giving the person every possible easy item. Instead, CAT-based scales gradually presented harder and harder items until the individual stops getting them all right. Likewise, if a person struggles with easy items, there is no need to give him or her every possible difficult item. This approach often results in better measurement with fewer items presented to the test taker.

Examples:

Regardless of the model used, the item functioning for each item can be shown graphically by charting the probability of getting an item correct based on varying ability levels. This type of graph is known as an **Item Characteristic Curve**. For example, the graph below shows item characteristic curves of multiple items evaluated using a one parameter (1PL) model. As shown in this figure, the slopes of the items are the same, but some items are more difficult than others. For item #1, the probability of getting the item correct is high, even at low ability levels. For item #3, only high ability individuals are likely to get the item correct.

Figure 16.1 - Example items for a 1 parameter model

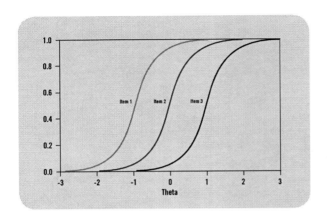

Next is an example of item characteristic curves with a two parameter model. All items have the same difficulty (i.e., about 50% of respondents get the item correct), but the slopes are different. In this case, the probability of getting item #1 correct gradually increases as ability level increases. In contrast, there is a much smaller range on theta in which the probability increases of getting item #3 correct. In this case, item #1 provides a small amount of information about a person's true score across a wide range of ability ranges whereas item #3 provides much more information within just a small ability range.

Figure 16.2 - Example items for a 2 parameter model

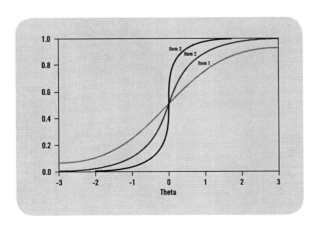

The amount of information provided by an item at different ability levels can also be shown graphically through IRT. This is known as the **Item Information Function**. The figure below provides an example. In this example, the first item provides a small amount of information across a wide ability range (similar to item #1 in Figure 16.2) and the second item provides a lot of information in a short ability range (similar to item #3 in Figure 16.2).

Figure 16.3 – Example items for item information function graphs

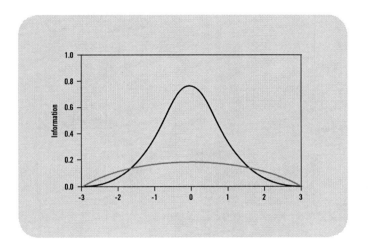

Finally, below is an example of item characteristic curves for a three parameter model (3PL). As shown in this graph, the ability to guess the correct answer, even at low ability levels, differs by item. Item #1 is likely a multiple choice item with only two answers, so that even those with very low ability levels have a 50% chance of guessing the correct answer. Item #2 represents an item with four possible answers, so that the chances of guessing the correct answer are 25%. Finally, there is very little chance (only 10%) that individuals with low ability levels will guess the correct answer on Item #3.

Figure 16.1 – Example items for a 3 parameter model

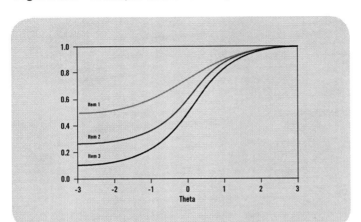

What to Watch For:

Most IRT analyses are not as complicated as people think, but it can be very confusing to those who are not familiar with the terms or who have no background or training in the basic concepts. The bottom line is that IRT provides a method for evaluating items in much more detail than most methods covered in other areas of this guide. As a result, IRT can often provide an effective method for developing very accurate tests that pinpoint a person's true ability level with the fewest possible items.

One of the biggest disadvantages of IRT is it often requires one to collect pilot data on hundreds of items from thousands of potential test takers. This works well for many standardized educational tests because thousands of individuals take these assessments each year and, consequently, can be used to pilot potential items for the next year's exam. However, this may not be possible for many I/O test publishers who either focus on specific populations or whose clients may demand short tests that cannot accommodate large pilot data collection efforts.

In general, IRT is much like meta-analysis in that it is very difficult to adequately summarize the topic in only a few short pages. Running IRT analyses not only requires extensive training, but access to large datasets and often expensive statistical programs.

Interpreting IRT results, however, does not need to be difficult when a person has a basic understanding of the fundamental concepts and terms.

Food for Thought:

CAT often provides a way to produce more accurate results while giving individual subjects fewer items. But, can you think of additional advantages (hint: especially those that result from giving different items to different test takers?)

Chapter 4

OTHER CONSIDERATIONS

The topics covered in this chapter are not statistical techniques, but are important for properly interpreting research results. Unfortunately, we are often presented with incorrect or misleading results and conclusions based on data collected using poor measures and research methods.

As such, this chapter represents a sort of hodgepodge of information that is always good to keep in the back of your mind. For example, anytime you see someone make claims about people from different cultures based on data collected in different languages, you should always be wary of whether or not the findings represent actual cultural differences or simply problems with translations. Likewise, information presented in sections covering item writing and study design is useful when trying to evaluate or understand measures created or research results reported by others.

TOPIC 17 WRITING ITEMS

Within I/O Psychology, most of the data we collect are gathered using items someone, at some point, wrote. Whether it be responses on a survey, items on an assessment, ratings of job performance, or nearly any other measurement where we ask someone to read an item and provide a response, the quality of data and results depend on the quality of the items.

Yet surprisingly, very few courses spend much time talking about how to write quality items. What makes this even more surprising is that anyone who tries to write items quickly realizes how difficult of a task it can be. And worse yet, estimates of the number of items a person has to write to get just one good one can range anywhere from 5 to more than 20. In short, writing quality items is often ignored but is critical to nearly everything we do in I/O Psychology.

Key terms:

- **Response rates** – How frequently individuals respond to different survey items.

- **Confidential** – Usually taken to mean that results from individual respondents will not be shared with anyone, although one might still collect information about the person when collecting data.

- **Anonymity** – When a researcher does not collect any identifying information from respondents (i.e., no personal information that could later be used to determine who provided what responses).

Examples:

One of the most difficult yet frequent activities I/O Psychologists perform is writing items used to evaluate an employee's performance. Any attempt to measure performance relies on accurate and reliable performance measures. Some general steps for writing performance items should include:

1. Find anything and everything that already exists. For example, if trying to measure job performance, one should look at what the organization they are working with has used to measure job performance in the past. Preexisting measures are not necessarily good ones, but they provide an idea of how others have attempted to define and measure job performance in the past.

2. Identify and talk to people who represent the intended target audience. Anytime a researcher collects data, they will eventually present results to others. If those others are inside a company, the researcher should make sure the terminology he or she uses makes sense to those in the company and that items cover all aspects of performance others might think are important. If the intended audience is an academic one (e.g., published results in a peer review journal), researchers should look at similar measures used in the past and be prepared to make an argument for why their new items are better.

3. Pilot test items prior to large scale data collection. One of the worst things researchers can do is collect data and then realize they should have used better items. Pilot testing items with a small sample first can help identify potentially confusing items and provide one with an idea of what to expect in terms of responses.

What to Watch For:

- Clarity of wording – obviously, items need to be clear and easy for others to understand. Pilot testing items with others is critical because what makes sense to the person writing an item might not make sense to others.

- Strength of wording – when writing items, adjectives matter. Item response rates can be influenced by word choice. For example, an individual who can "effectively" manage their task might not necessarily be "good" at managing their tasks.

- Avoid double meanings – a person writing an item knows the intended meaning of the item, but others reading the item might not. For example, "works well with customers" could mean customers generally tend to like an employee, that the employee deals well with customer complaints, or the employee is good at getting customers to commit to a sale.

- Avoid double loadings or "double barreled items" – the best items are those that ask about only one thing. For example, when writing an item to assess interpersonal skills, one shouldn't ask something such as "enjoys interacting with and works well with coworkers." The fact is, some people might enjoy interacting with coworkers but are not very good at it (or vice versa). If both enjoying interactions with coworkers and being good at it are important, they should be addressed using two separate items.

- Variance is important – an item that produces very similar results for everyone is usually not a very useful item. Both items and response formats need to be written so respondents are realistically likely to use a variety of response options.

- Items should always match their stem (if using one) – not all items require a stem, but when a researcher uses item stems, they need to make sure every item flows well and makes grammatical sense according to that stem. For example, an item stem of "How often does this employee:" works fine for "meet his or her goals" but not for "demonstrates exceptional job performance."

- Items should always match their rating scale – unfortunately, people mess this one up all of the time. For example, if asking behavioral items (e.g., "this person reaches all of his or her goals), the rating scale should be behavioral or frequency based (e.g., "never," "sometimes," or "always"). Behavioral items often don't work as well with agreement scales. After all, if a person does always reach his or her goals, should the respondent "agree" or "strongly agree" with this statement. What if the employee only rarely misses a goal? Should that individual receive a rating of disagree simply because he or she missed one goal one time? Finally, avoid using frequency related items with frequency related response formats. An item like "this person usually reaches all of his or her goals" doesn't make sense with response options like "sometimes." After all, what does it mean if someone sometimes usually reaches his or her goals?

Food for Thought:

What problems or potential issues can you identify in the following examples?

Rate the employee's performance from 1 (needs improvement) to 5 (exceptional) in each of the following areas:

This employee:

1.	Works well with others	☐ 1	☐ 2	☐ 3	☐ 4	☐ 5
2.	Always meets his or her goals	☐ 1	☐ 2	☐ 3	☐ 4	☐ 5
3.	Is loyal to the company	☐ 1	☐ 2	☐ 3	☐ 4	☐ 5
4.	A good team player	☐ 1	☐ 2	☐ 3	☐ 4	☐ 5
5.	Is detailed and accurate in his or her work	☐ 1	☐ 2	☐ 3	☐ 4	☐ 5

Rate the degree to which you agree with the following statements:

1.	My company cares about its employees.	☐ Disagree	☐ Neutral	☐ Agree
2.	My boss and coworkers are good at what they do.	☐ Disagree	☐ Neutral	☐ Agree
3.	Employees are treated fairly at my company.	☐ Disagree	☐ Neutral	☐ Agree
4.	I have the resources I need.	☐ Disagree	☐ Neutral	☐ Agree
5.	I enjoy working for my company.	☐ Disagree	☐ Neutral	☐ Agree

TOPIC 18 TRANSLATIONS

Translating any item from one language to another may seem relatively simple. After all, one should be able to find anyone fluent in both languages (i.e., their original language and the new "target" language) and just have that person create a translation. And, in some cases, it can be that simple. But, it often takes a lot of time and effort to develop quality translations, especially when the content of the item involves more than simply translating individual words from one language to another.

Easy translations typically come only in the form of basic demographics, such as name, gender, years on the job, etc. But even with demographics, translations can quickly become more complex with common items such as those assessing race/ethnicity (which varies by country), job title (where different titles mean different things in different regions), or industry (which is often viewed differently in different areas of the world). Even age can be tricky because in some Asian cultures, individuals are considered "1" when they are first born.

Moreover, most of the items within the world of I/O Psychology are much more complex than basic demographics. For example, all of the considerations outlined in the previous topic (Topic #17 – writing items) become big potential problems when translating an item from one language to another.

Key terms:

- **Forward translation** – When one or more individuals conduct an initial translation of items from one language to another.

- **Back/backward translation** – When another person or individual then translates those new items back to the original language. This is often a useful way of identifying any problems in item content or meaning that might have resulted from the initial forward translation.

- **Application** – When one tries to translate an item into a new language as literally as possible (i.e., have the item say the exact same thing in the new language).

- **Adaptation** – When a translator makes modifications to an item during the translation process, as needed, to try to ensure cultural relevance.

- **Assembly** – When rather than conducting direct translations, a translator writes new items intended to measure the same construct, although item wording and content might be different.

Examples:

Although there are multiple processes one might use to develop new translations of an item, most effective processes share the same general characteristics:

1. Involve multiple people in the process.

2. Translators need to not only be fluent in both languages, but familiar with both cultures and the content of the items. For example, it is often best to have someone with an HR background involved in the process of translating job-related items or someone with a psychological background involved in the process of translating items regarding personality, attitudes, etc.

3. Pilot test with a new group once initial translations are complete. One should also follow-up with this pilot group by asking questions such as whether or not they saw any potential issues with item wording, grammar, content, etc. These questions should be as specific as possible (i.e., not just if reviewers thought the items were okay).

What to Watch For:

To help aid in the translation process, initial item writers should try to avoid idioms (e.g., "toot your own horn," or "if it feels good do it") because they are often difficult to translate into other languages. Also, unless a scale is designed to measure any of these specific topics, it is often best to avoid questions that might not go over as well in some cultures compared to others (e.g., politics, religion, topics related to valuing diversity, etc.).

Even the most thorough translation process will sometimes result in new items that aren't as effective or don't measure the same exact thing as the original. For this reason, translation should always be considered an ongoing process. It is the responsibility of test publishers to regularly analyze items (e.g., checking for things like similar response rates with similar samples) to make sure items are working properly. Furthermore, it is the responsibility of those using items to make sure the test publisher follows some sort of process for regularly evaluating and maintaining item translations.

Food for Thought:

What are some potential issues with the following personality-related items?

1. I like big cities more than the country.

2. On the weekends, I am often a couch potato.

3. I rarely get upset with other people.

4. I am always cold.

5. I often think my country is moving in the wrong direction.

6. I believe religion is more important than politics.

7. I enjoy traveling to other countries.

8. I take pride in being a good follower.

9. I am easily excited.

10. I enjoy spending time alone.

TOPIC 19 STUDY DESIGN

The key to any good study is proper design. And while every study is different, all share key components that one should be aware of prior to collecting data.

Key terms:

- **Observational study** – Studies that collect data from individuals in ways that are not supposed to affect them (e.g., surveys, on-site observations).

- **Experiments** – Studies that impose one or more treatments or conditions on study participants.

- **Experimental group** – The group(s) that receives certain treatments (e.g., a new drug, specific instructions).

- **Control group** – The group that does not receive any treatments so it may serve as a comparison or base rate group.

- **Random sampling** – Randomly selecting study participants out of a total possible subject pool.

- **Stratified sampling** – Selecting a certain number of participants with specific characteristics from a total possible subject pool. For example, if a researcher wants to study college freshmen, he or she might specifically sample a certain percentage of participants from different major areas to make sure all are represented.

- **Sample characteristics** – The characteristics of the sample used to collect data can have a dramatic impact on a study's results. Some potential problems with sample characteristics are obvious (e.g., one wouldn't want to conduct an employee opinion survey for a company but only collect data from one department while leaving others out entirely).

- **Representation** – How well a sample reflects the intended population of interest in terms of critical sample characteristics.

- **Attrition** – When subjects drop out during the course of a study. Attrition not only results in smaller sample sizes, but often raises issues over whether or not those who drop out are different in some important way from those who do not drop out.

- **Response bias** – Unfortunately, people don't necessarily read or interpret items exactly the same way. This can be especially problematic when individuals respond to items like those on climate/culture surveys or job performance ratings, because some people tend to be more lenient or more critical than others.

- **Generalizability** – How well results from one study or sample can be expected to apply to other samples. In other words, can one expect that results would be similar for other samples?

Examples:

Although this list is not all inclusive, here are several things to ask about when reviewing research results presented by others.

1. What are the primary research questions?

2. What is the ideal sample to address these questions?

3. Did the sample used for data collection reflect this ideal sample as closely as possible?

4. What are the ideal measures to address the research questions?

5. Did the measures used to collect data reflect these ideal measures as closely as possible?

6. What potential confounding variables were examined?

7. What potential confounding variables were unaccounted for?

8. Were appropriate data analyses used?

9. Were results reported in a manner that was clear and accurate?

10. What steps were taken to ensure accuracy in data collection and analyses?

11. Who is the primary intended audience?

12. Were results presented in a manner that was effective for this audience?

What to Watch For:

Experiments are designed to try to get at cause-and-effect relationships. Observational studies are not. Don't be fooled by results from observational studies that are presented as displaying cause/effect relationships.

Also, there are some statistical methods for controlling for response bias (often called **rater effects** when used to describe different biases individuals have when rating the performance of others), but these methods are typically only useful when a respondent rates several targets, such as a supervisor providing ratings for three or more subordinates. Another way to help with response bias is through **Frame of Reference (FOR) training**, where a researcher provides detailed instructions to raters concerning what each potential response option means (e.g., examples of what good teamwork is versus bad teamwork). Finally, **Behavioral Anchored Rating Scales (BARS)** are another method of trying to reduce rater error/response bias. With BARS, specific examples of behaviors representing different ratings are provided to respondents to illustrate what different points on the rating scale represent.

Food for Thought:

We have all seen a picture of Harry Truman holding up the Chicago Tribune headline from the day after the election proclaiming "Dewey Defeats Truman," but misleading political polls existed long before the 1948 presidential election (and, unfortunately, continue to exist today). One famous early example occurred prior to the 1936 presidential election between Alf Landon and Franklin Roosevelt. A popular weekly magazine, the Literary Digest, included a survey that readers could mail back on a post card. Of their 10 million or so readers at the time, over 2 million responded, a truly astronomical number for any poll, even today. Based on these results, they concluded Landon would win by a landslide. What might have been wrong with this survey?

TOPIC 20 PRESENTING YOUR OWN RESULTS

This section covers a few remaining thoughts worth taking into consideration when reviewing data provided by others or presenting your own results.

- Garbage In Garbage Out (GIGO). Most people have heard of this term/phrase and there is certainly nothing profound in it. But, it is worth noting none-the-less. Basically, without good quality data to start with, results are pretty much meaningless. Even the slightest miscalculation or misalignment of data (e.g., failing to match up people's predictor scores with the correct outcomes) can throw off a study's results entirely.

- Don't take everything at face value. Hopefully, the outlines of what to look for and examples of misleading statistics presented throughout this guide already make this point. But, even when presented with results that don't seem extraordinary, it is worth always looking at things with a critical eye. Key things to look at are data quality, methods used to collect and analyze data, and the potential exclusion of things like confounding variables.

- When results don't look correct, they probably aren't. When you fully expect results to work out in a certain way and they don't, don't panic. The fact of the matter is, very unusual or odd looking results are the result of some sort of error at least 90% of the time. Granted, we sometimes find results we don't expect, which can be an exciting part of the research and discovery process. But, you should always double check your analyses and results. This is particularly true when your results seem odd or unexpected. In other words, if a result simply looks wrong, more often than not, it is wrong.

- You probably don't need to be a statistical expert, but you might need access to one. At least within the world of I/O Psychology, most people have training on the techniques covered in the first two chapters of this guide. The bad news is that means when interacting with I/O folks, you might be expected to have the same basic understanding of these concepts and techniques. The good news is you also probably have, or can quickly find access to others who can lend you a hand. So, when you need help, ask for it. In particular, many of the topics covered in the last two chapters require much more specialized training that is often only obtained through one or more graduate school courses dedicated entirely to the topic or through years of experience working in the area. In other words, very few people are experts in these areas and you should not, therefore, expect to quickly become one yourself. Instead, if you need help with these topics, find an expert. Luckily, many people in the I/O community not only know one another but are quite nice when it comes to lending their expertise to others.

- Get to know your data. One mistake many researchers make is to immediately begin running analyses (e.g., correlations, regressions, ANOVAs) as soon as they have a full dataset without first looking at their data. Before conducting an analysis on any variable, spend a little bit of time looking at the data for that variable. Look for potential outliers on either the lowest or highest end of a scale. Look for missing data. Look at the distribution of scores on each variable to see if anything else stands out as potentially wrong or problematic. When running correlations, look at a scatter plot to see if scores from one or two subjects clearly stand out from the rest. These basic reviews will not only help you become more familiar with your data, but are the best way to identify potential mistakes in the data that can throw off your results entirely.

In terms of presenting results to others, there are a few critical considerations you should always keep in mind:

- Know your audience – One of the biggest mistakes people make when presenting results to others is failing to take their audience into account. Before putting together a results presentation, identify your intended audience. Find out what their level of statistical sophistication is and prepare your materials accordingly. Perhaps even more importantly, find out ahead of time what they want to know. Along those lines, you might need to be prepared to present results in different ways to different audiences. For example, when writing up results for a more academically inclined audience, clear details concerning your specific research questions, research strategy, sample, analyses, and results all matter. In contrast, when presenting results to a group of executives, only the briefest of study descriptions might be needed. Instead, executives often want to focus on results and their meaning.

- Be ready with a good summary – With any results presentation, a good abstract or executive summary is often the most important piece you will create. The fact is, your summary is all most people will read. As a result, it should briefly cover all major aspects of your study including methods, results, and a brief overview of what your results should mean to intended audience members.

- Don't skimp on interpretation – If you are presenting results to others, whether you feel like it or not, you are the expert. As such, be prepared to tell your audience what you think your results mean. Especially early in their careers, many researchers tend to focus too much on the details of a study and leave it to their audience to draw their own conclusions. Don't be afraid to explain to your audience why you think your results are important to them.

- Use tables and figures when possible – If you can summarize your results in a table or figure, do. Even journal article reviewers often recommend presenting results through tables and figures when possible. This not only helps put results into perspective, but is often easier on the reader. As a cautionary note, make sure that tables and figures are straight forward and easy to understand. Anyone with a basic understanding of a study should be able to look at a table or figure and quickly and easily understand the information presented.

- Keep things simple – It is often best to focus on one or two key points when presenting results. As with a good summary, a presentation should focus on just what is important to intended audience members and what those results mean to them.

- Aesthetics matter – The ability to conduct good research and present results in a visually appealing manner are two entirely separate and unrelated skills. As with running your own analyses, if you do not have a lot of experience with creating white papers or presentations, find someone who does and ask them for help.

- Don't be afraid to say you don't know the answer to a question – Especially when presenting results in front of others, most of us dread the possibility of being asked questions we don't know the answer to. But, the best strategy is often the simplest, say that you don't know but will find out and get back to the person. Often the worst thing you can do in this situation is back yourself into a corner by saying something that doesn't end up being true. Furthermore, most people will appreciate it if you follow-up with them later because it shows you care about their question and them as an audience member. In other words, saying you don't know but will find out is often a good way of turning a potential negative situation into a positive one.

- Practice – The best way to make sure you are ready to present results to others is to have at least one or two people who represent your intended audience review your results first. If you are submitting something for publication, ask some experienced researchers to review your manuscript before submitting it to a journal. If you are presenting results to a client, practice first using someone around you who will provide honest and constructive feedback. When conducting research, most of us are too close to the study ourselves to anticipate what questions others might have or what others might find confusing. The best way to prepare for these questions and avoid problems concerning potentially confusing results is to have others review your materials first.

INDEX/KEY TERMS

Adaptation	98	Dummy variable	41
Alpha	20	Effect size	20
Alternative hypothesis	19	Eigenvalue	60
ANCOVA	49	Endogenous variable	68
Anonymity	93	Error	25
ANOVA	49	Error term (in SEM)	68
Application	97	Exogenous variable	68
Assembly	98	Expected frequencies	53
Assessment	II	Experiment	101
Association	35	Experimental group	101
Attrition	102	Exploratory factor analysis (EFA)	59
Back/backward translation	97	External validity	31
Bare bones meta-analysis	74	Face validity	30
Behavioral anchored rating scales (BARS)	103	Factor	59
Bell curve	13	File drawer problem	77
Beta weight	40	Fit Indices	67
Bi-modal	3	Fixed Parameter	68
Categorical variable	9	Forward translation	97
Causation	35	Frame of reference training	103
CFI	69	Free Parameter	68
Change in R-Square	42	Frequency	3
Chi-square	53	Full mediation	79
Chi-square (in SEM)	68	Generalizability	102
Classical test theory (CTT)	83	Goodness of fit	53
Coefficient alpha	26	Hierarchical regression	42
Computer Adaptive Test (CAT)	85	Histogram	13
Concurrent validity	31	Hypothesis testing	19
Confidence interval	26	Independent samples t-test	45
Confidence interval	75	Independent variable	III
Confidential	93	Inferential statistics	19
Confirmatory Factor Analysis (CFA)	67	Interaction	49
Confounding variable	III	Interaction effect	49
Constrained Parameter	68	Intercept	39
Construct	II	Internal validity	31
Construct validity	30	Interquartile range	3
Content validity	30	Interval scale	9
Continuous variable	9	Item	II
Control group	101	Item characteristics curve	85
Control variable	41	Item information function	87
Convergent validity	31	Item response theory (IRT)	83
Correlation	35	Item writing	93
Covariance	36	k	74
Covariate	41	Kuder-Richardson Formula (KR-20)	26
Credibility interval	76	Kurtosis	15
Criterion variable	29	Lagrange multiplier	69
Criterion-related validity	31	Likert scale	10
Cross-loading	61	Logistic regression	41
Cumulative frequency	3	Low base rates	55
Curvilinear relationships	42	Main effect	49
d-score	46	MANCOVA	50
Degrees of freedom	21	MANOVA	50
Dependent variable	III	Mean	3
Descriptive statistics	3	Mean split	3
difference score	46	Measure	II
Discriminant validity	31	Measures of Central Tendency	3
Distribution	13	Median	3

Median split	3	Regression	39
Mediation	79	Relative frequency	3
Meta-analysis	73	Reliability	25
Mode	3	Repeated measures t-test	46
Model modification	69	Representation	101
Moderation	79	Response bias	102
Moderator (in meta-analysis)	75	Response rates	93
Multi-dimensional	27	RMSEA	69
Multi-modal	3	Rotation	61
Multicolinearity	44	Sample	II
Multiple regression	40	Sample bias	II
N	74	Sample characteristics	101
Nominal scale	9	Sample size	II
Normal distribution	13	Sampling error	II
Null hypothesis	19	Scale	II
Oblique solution	60	Scatter plots	36
Observational study	101	Scree plot	60
Observed effect size	74	Simple regression	40
Observed frequencies	53	Skew/Skewness	15
Observed score	25	Slope	39
Observed validity	74	Spearman's rho	36
One-sample t-test	45	Split forms reliability	26
One-tailed test	20	SRMR	69
Operational effect size	74	Standard deviation	3
Operational validity	74	Standard error of measurement	25
Ordinal scale	9	Standard error of the mean	26
Orthogonal solution	60	Standardized score	14
Outcome variable	29	Statistical artifacts	74
Outlier	15	Statistical significance	20
Paired samples t-test	46	Stepwise regression	40
Parallel forms reliability	26	Stratified sampling	101
Parameter (in SEM)	68	Structural Equation Modeling (SEM)	67
Partial mediation	80	Study design	101
Path analysis	67	t-test	45
Percentage of variance accounted for by artifacts	75	Test	II
		Test-retest reliability	26
Percentile scores	10	Theta (in IRT)	84
Person product-moment	36	Translations	97
Phi Coefficient	36	True effect size	75
Point-biserial	36	True score	25
Population	II	True validity	75
Post hoc test	49	Two-tailed test	20
Power	21	Type 1 error	20
Practical significance	20	Type 2 error	20
Predictive validity	31	Types of scales	9
Predictor variable	29	Utility	29
Principle Components Analysis (PCA)	60	Utility Analysis	30
Probability	21	Validation	29
Random sampling	101	Validity	29
Range restriction	37	Variable	II
Rasch model	84	Variance	3
Rater effects	103	Walt test	69
Ratio scale	10	z-score	14
Raw scores	10		

APPENDIX

Comments concerning each of the

"Food for Thought" sections for most Topic areas

Topic #1 – Why do most accidents happen close to home?

This is likely true, but it doesn't necessarily mean we are less vigilant when driving close to home. Instead, we simply may have more accidents close to home because most of our driving occurs close to home.

Topic #2 – Do teenagers have fewer fatal accidents than individuals in their 20's?

Again, this certainly appears to be true, but it doesn't take into account how much teenagers drive compared to individuals of other ages. In other words, accidents per miles driven is a better indicator of driving ability than accidents per person. The graph below provides those results.

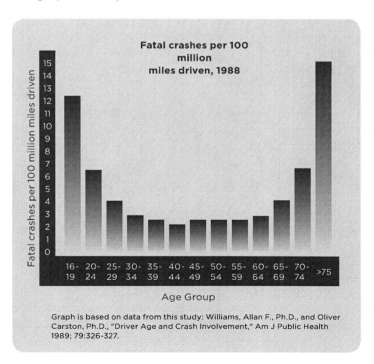

Graph is based on data from this study: Williams, Allan F., Ph.D., and Oliver Carston, Ph.D., "Driver Age and Crash Involvement," Am J Public Health 1989; 79:326-327.

Topic #3 – How can we have record high temperatures across the year with thousands of examples of record lows?

This is simply a matter of outliers. By definition, outliers do not occur that often, but they do occur. If one were to look at all low temperatures for all 20,000 plus cities in the U.S. for every day of the year, there will inevitably be thousands of examples of new record lows even if the average temperature across the entire country increases slightly.

Topic #4 – What are problems with failures to replicate significant results?

There is no surprise here that one might find significant results even if the effect they are testing either doesn't exist or is small in magnitude. What is a bit more concerning, however, is that non-significant results often have a more difficult time making it into peer reviewed publications. So, if by random chance, a researcher finds significant results and publishes them, it is much harder for those who cannot replicate the results of the previous study to publish their results. In fact, at least one researcher claimed to have been rejected by the Journal of Personality and Social Psychology for a study where he failed to replicate Dr. Bern's results because, at least in part, Dr. Bern was one of the reviewers. True or not, many experts in a given field often serve as reviewers for topics in that same field, which can make it even more difficult to publish studies with results that contradict previous research. Of even bigger concern, however, are all of the results we are flooded with each day that no one, especially the person presenting them, has ever tried to replicate.

Topic #5 – What does it mean to get a higher alpha with fewer teamwork items?

The problem here is that the alpha is so high for the two items ("Is a good team player" and "Works well in a team") because they essentially measure the exact same thing. Granted, both are important indicators of teamwork, but additional items such as "Is friendly and cooperative" might also be an indicator of teamwork, but as an indication of how well someone works with people outside of his or her specific team. So, if the intent is to just measure how well someone works on a specific team, the simpler two-item measure might work fine. But, if the concept of "teamwork" is intended to measure how well a person works with others in a company outside of his or her team, additional items might be important even if they lower alpha to some degree. This example shows that someone can artificially inflate alpha by writing items that ask the same thing in slightly different ways. That doesn't mean, however, that it will result in a scale that measures everything it is intended to measure.

Topic #6 – Is the Oxford Capacity Analysis (OCA) valid?

One could argue that the answer to both questions is "yes." As many opponents argue, there is little evidence that the OCA accurately measures one's personality. So, if the intent is to measure personality, then it is not likely a very valid assessment (or at least evidence to the fact isn't strong). But, remember that validity concerns whether or not a scale or assessment does what it is supposed to do. If the intended purpose of the OCA is to provide information useful for recruiting purposes within the Church of Scientology, it is unlikely it would continue to be so widely used unless it provided information that helps recruit people to the church. So, based on this view of validity (i.e., is it useful as a recruiting tool?), the OCA is likely quite valid.

Topic #7 – Autism, churches and bars, and the most predictive selection instrument of all time

The first two examples likely suffer from the same problem, where there is a confounding variable of some sort that actually produces the correlation between the two variables under examination. For example, better exposure to health care might increase both the number of vaccines administered each year and the number of children diagnosed with Autism (in fact there is a correlation between number of vaccines and many childhood diagnoses). For the second example, the confounding variable is the size of the town. The fact is, one would get the same result if replacing churches and/or bars with other common institutions such as gas stations, grocery stories, etc.

The third example is something we unfortunately see a lot in I/O Psychology. The term for what is happening is "capitalizing on sampling error." In other words, one would expect at least 5% of the items (10) to be significant due to random chance. Assuming that some items are actually related to job performance, it is no surprise that 20 out of 200 came out as statistically significant. But, it is highly unlikely that all of these items actually are significantly correlated with job performance. As a result, it is also highly unlikely these results will replicate to future samples. Long story short, always be cautious of predictive validity coefficients derived from single samples. As covered under Topic #4, replication is essential.

Topic #8 – Does EQ predict 85% of job performance?

The problem is that IQ and EQ are not the only possible variables that influence job performance. Even if job performance could be measured perfectly (see Topic #5), there are countless other variables that influence our work behaviors and, consequently, our performance on the job. Some of the most common include experience, training, motivation, and the availability of necessary resources. So, while IQ might account for 15% of the variance in job performance, no one other variable accounts for the remaining 85%.

Topic #9 – Does higher state spending on students result in lower SAT scores?

Colleges in many states do not require the SAT. Instead, many use the ACT (especially in the middle of the nation). North Dakota, in particular, favors the ACT (see below). So, only students likely to apply to universities that are far away are likely to take the SAT in North Dakota. As it turns out, many of those students do so because they are the best and brightest and, therefore, are more attracted to prestigious universities with higher admission standards; universities that, as it turns out, are also more likely to require the SAT.

SAT Scores, 1998			
State	Verbal	Math	Participation Rate
North Dakota	590	599	5%
New Jersey	497	508	79%

Topic #10 – What are the implications of a cross-over interaction?

As this example shows, failing to include important variables can dramatically influence the results a researcher gets and, consequently, how they interpret those results. For example, in this case, what would have happened if the individual conducting the study failed to take the initial message into account? If the person initiating the conversation always approached a person by introducing themselves, the results would indicate that keeping one's distance was preferable to being to close. However, if the person initiating the conversation always approached a person by asking the person's name, a researcher might reach the exact opposite conclusion (i.e., that being close was better than keeping one's distance).

Topic #11 – How can there be a female bias in admission rates when a higher percentage of males are admitted overall?

The reason the results indicate a female bias when broken out by department is that a greater percentage of women apply for departments with much lower pass rates. So, even though women tend to do just as well or better in most departments, not nearly as many apply to departments with high admission rates. Instead, women are simply much more likely than men to apply to departments with low admission rates, bringing their overall admission percentage down.

Topic #12 – Do items measuring how quick a person is to make decisions represent a one or two factor solution?

The fact is, either solution works pretty well here. Based on the two factor approach, there clearly appears to be two different sets of items. The first set of items (1-3) measures how spontaneous a person is while the second measures how much attention a person gives to specific details (items 4-6). The "correct" solution, therefore, likely depends on what one is trying to measure in terms of how they define making quick decisions. It would appear as though the first set of items get at this most directly, so a reasonable conclusion would be to retain just those three items. However, if the purpose of this scale is to also indicate how much time a person spends on specific details, an argument could easily be made to also keep the last three items. Given the high factor loadings for all six items on the one factor solution, the ultimate decision comes down to whether or not one believes the items measuring attention to details accurately represent an important part of the general construct (i.e., quickness to make decisions) under examination.

Topic #13 – What are the implications of including a large number of variables in an SEM model?

The first is obvious based on the information provided in Topic #13: the more variables one has in a model, the more data he or she needs to test the model. The second, however, is less obvious. Because modification indices are based on statistical tests, the more potential modifications one can make (i.e., the more variables and, consequently, more potential paths in a model), the greater the likelihood that one could overfit their data if relying too much on results from Wald and Lagrange Multiplier results. In other words, out of 200 potential modifications to a model, about 10 will show up as statistically significant simply due to random chance (at an alpha level of .05). So in general, the more variables included in a model, the more cautious one should be about making modifications to a model.

Topic #14 – What is the problem with low correlations among scales intended to measure Conscientiousness?

The problem is that if the scales are not highly related to one another, it is likely that they are actually measuring different things. When conducting a meta-analysis to evaluate the relationship between any predictor measure and an outcome of interest, results will only be meaningful if the predictor measure is consistent across studies.

One way to deal with this is to run separate meta-analyses for each predictor to see if your results are consistent. Or, if you have a variety of predictor variables but your results consistently show that 100% of the variance in your results is accounted for by statistical artifacts, you can be reasonably sure that your results are at least consistent across your predictors. But, another often better way to account for this is to focus only on studies that use the same predictor. Of course, this only works when you have enough samples available for any one predictor.

Topic #15 – How can safety climate be both a mediator and a moderator?

Safety climate has been found to mediate the relationship between individual characteristics and safety performance. As outlined in the SEM example provided under Topic #13, certain individual characteristics predict safety related behaviors. The same is true for the individual characteristics of managers because management behaviors, in large part, determine what an organization's climate will look like. So, managers who are cautious and careful and, therefore, more likely to promote and encourage safe behaviors, can influence safety outcomes. But they do so by establishing an environment that encourages and rewards safe performance. Therefore, the relationship between management characteristics and safety outcomes is, at least in part, mediated by safety climate.

But, safety climate can also be a moderator, particularly for entry level employees. For example, high levels of risk taking often results in more accidents and injuries. For that reason, risk taking is predictive of safety outcomes. But it is more predictive of safety outcomes in environments in which safety isn't stressed, meaning that people are more open to (and perhaps even encouraged to) take risks. In contrast, there is less of a relationship between risk taking and safety outcomes in highly structured or safety conscientious environments, where individuals have less opportunity to take risks. In this way, safety climate moderates the relationships between risk taking and safety outcomes where this relationship is higher in a climate that doesn't emphasize safety than it is one in which safety is regularly monitored and emphasized.

Topic #16 – What are additional advantages of Computer Adaptive Testing (CAT)?

Another primary advantage of CAT relates to cheating and test security. It is much harder for individuals to cheat on a test when they don't know what items they will be given (and don't even have access to the full set of items that comprise a test). Along those lines, CAT makes it easier for test publishers to keep their scoring logic from leaking out to potential test takers. With static tests, where test takers always receive the same items, one can eventually collect enough data to determine how those items are scored to create individual scales. This is more difficult with CAT because no one individual test taker receives the exact same set of items.

Topic #17 – Problems with items.

There are several problems throughout these items. Some examples include:

1. The item "Works well with others" is a bit problematic because "others" can be a lot of different people. It would be better to ask specifically about working well with customers, coworkers, etc. In other words, this item could mean different things to different raters.

2. The same could be said for "I have the resources I need" because resources can mean different things to different people and for "Is detailed and accurate in his or her work" because being detailed and accurate could be two different things.

3. The item "A good team player" does not follow the stem "This employee".

4. The item "My boss and coworkers are good at what they do" is double loaded in that it asks about two different things (the employee's boss and the employee's coworkers).

5. The item "Always meets his or her goals" does not fit with the rating scale (needs improvement – exceptional). It is basically just a yes/no item.

6. The item "Is loyal to the company" isn't too bad, but the fact is, there is no way to really know what another person is thinking. A better item might be "Displays loyalty to the company."

Topic #18 – Items that pose potential translation problems.

Here is a brief description of at least one potential problem with each of the items provided as examples:

1. I like big cities more than the country – Individual perceptions of what is a big city and what is the country can differ by culture.

2. On the weekends, I am often a couch potato – Not everyone knows what the phrase "couch potato" means.

3. I rarely get upset with other people – The word "upset" can easily be translated in a way that varies in terms of item strength (e.g., unhappy versus angry).

4. I am always cold – The problem here is a potential double meaning, where "cold" could refer to physical coldness or coldness towards others.

5. I often think my country is moving in the wrong direction – This item might not be politically appropriate in some countries.

6. I believe religion is more important than politics – This item asks about religion and politics, both of which might not be appropriate in some countries.

7. I enjoy traveling to other countries – Foreign travel is both easier and more common in some countries than others.

8. I take pride in being a good follower – The term "follower" might be translated inappropriately (e.g., "stalker"). In this case, a good back translation should reveal any major problems.

9. I am easily excited – Same as above but with the word "excited" in this one. Again, a good back translation should reveal any major problems.

10. I enjoy spending time alone – Same thing here in terms of how a translator might interpret the phrase "spend time alone."

Topic #19 – Literary Digest Presidential Election Poll

The *Literary Digest* poll seemed to have everything with over 2 million respondents. But, as it turned out, it was a very biased sample despite being so large. In general, the sample was over-representative of people with enough discretionary income (something not overly common in the 1930s) to afford both buy the *Literary Digest* and the willingness to fork up the necessary postage to mail the survey cards back to the magazine. As a result, it lacked a high percentage of likely Roosevelt voters.